Sewing

Fun Weekend Projects

Hearts-All-Around Neck Roll, page 121

hinkler

Sewing

Cover design: Hinkler Books Studio
Prepress: Graphic Print Group

hinkler

Published in 2013 by Hinkler Books Pty Ltd
45–55 Fairchild Street
Heatherton Victoria 3202 Australia
www.hinkler.com.au

ISBN: 978 1 7435 2062 8

Printed and bound in China

Originally published by
Company's Coming Publishing Limited
2311-96 Street
Edmonton, Alberta, Canada T6N 1G3
Tel: 780-450-6223   Fax: 780-450-1857
www.companyscoming.com

THE COMPANY'S COMING STORY

Jean Paré grew up with an understanding that family, friends and home cooking are the key ingredients for a good life. A mother of four, Jean worked as a professional caterer for 18 years, operating out of her home kitchen. During that time, she came to appreciate quick and easy recipes that call for everyday ingredients. In answer to mounting requests for her recipes, Company's Coming cookbooks were born, and Jean moved on to a new chapter in her career.

In the beginning, Jean worked from a spare bedroom in her home, located in the small prairie town of Vermilion, Alberta, Canada. The first Company's Coming cookbook, *150 Delicious Squares*, was an immediate bestseller. Today, with well over 150 titles in print, Company's Coming has earned the distinction of publishing Canada's most popular cookbooks. The company continues to gain new supporters by adhering to Jean's "Golden Rule of Cooking"—Never share a recipe you wouldn't use yourself. It's an approach that has worked—millions of times over!

Company's Coming cookbooks are distributed throughout Canada, the United States, Australia and other international English-language markets. French and Spanish language editions have also been published. Sales to date have surpassed 25 million copies with no end in sight. Familiar and trusted in home kitchens around the world, Company's Coming cookbooks are highly regarded both as

Company's Coming founder Jean Paré

kitchen workbooks and as family heirlooms.

Just as Company's Coming continues to promote the tradition of home cooking, the same is now true with crafting. Like good cooking, great craft results depend upon easy-to-follow instructions, readily available materials and enticing photographs of the finished products. Also like cooking, crafting is meant to be enjoyed in the home or cottage. Company's Coming Crafts, then, is a natural extension from the kitchen into the family room or den.

Because Company's Coming operates a test kitchen and not a craft shop, we've partnered with a major North American craft content publisher to assemble a variety of craft compilations exclusively for us. Our editors have been involved every step of the way. You can see the excellent results for yourself in the book you're holding.

Company's Coming Crafts are for everyone— whether you're a beginner or a seasoned pro. What better gift could you offer than something you've made yourself? In these hectic days, people still enjoy crafting parties; they bring family and friends together in the same way a good meal does. Company's Coming is proud to support crafters with this new creative book series.

We hope you enjoy these easy-to-follow, informative and colourful books, and that they inspire your creativity! So, don't delay—get crafty!

TABLE OF CONTENTS

Table Fashions

Stitch fashionable table wear to turn any meal into a fine dining experience. Create runners, toppers, baskets and placemats.

For Your Baby

Sew lovely nursery accessories for that special baby. Stitch blankets, toys, wraps, bags and bibs.

Sewing Room Accents

Highlight your sewing room with these practical and pretty designs. Make covers, pincushions, organizers and caddies.

Puppy Love, page 56

Quacker Cutie Bath Wrap, page 50

Twisted Basket & Quilted Table Topper, page 20

Autumn Leaves, page 34

Sewing Room Accessories, page 69

TABLE OF CONTENTS

For the Kitchen

Brighten your kitchen with attractive accents. Stitch tea cozies, mitts, blankets, covers and carriers.

Pillow Talk

Sew creative pillows to add the finishing touch. Use shirred cording, raggedy edges, bias strips and tufts.

Bags on the Go

Stitch stylish bags that coordinate with your wardrobe or fit many occasions. Try barrel bags, totes, evenings bags and wristlets.

Store & Serve Plate Caddies, page 98

Makeup in a Minute, page 145

Pillow Trio, page 102

Denim Delight, page 127

FOREWORD

Every day is a good day to sew for your home, for your friends and for yourself. Whether you are stitching table fashions, baby items, sewing-room accessories, accents for the kitchen, creative pillows or those irresistible bags, any day you can spend time sewing is a fun and rewarding day. In this book, we've selected 72 projects that will delight you.

One of the hottest trends in table fashions is runners. Table runners are quick to make, so quick in fact, that you can make one for every season. Placemats are even quicker. With today's fabrics, creative table covers are easy to make.

Decorating a baby nursery for your precious little one with a baby quilt, diaper stacker, bumper pads, organizers and soft toys make the nursery a delightful place to be. Diaper bags, bibs and wraps for bath time are other easy-to-sew items to make.

To make your sewing time more enjoyable, we've included projects for your sewing room. Sew a cover for your sewing machine and serger, a pocket organizer and basket. Delightful pincushions and an armchair caddy make your hand sewing easier.

A cheerful tea cozy, hot mats, dish towels and a bread basket will add colourful accents to your kitchen. For a relaxing picnic, stitch a blanket, flatware carrier and wine-bottle cover. Sewing beats cooking, but sewing for your kitchen is fun.

Almost any room of your home can use a pillow. They brighten any space, are soft and welcoming to use

and can reflect your own personal style and colours. Pillows add a lovely finishing touch to any room.

Cutting and sewing your own purses and bags offer every sewer the opportunity to make a design that is just the right size and shape. Stitch a drawstring bag, hobo-style bag, practical totes, classic evening purses and fun cellphone bags. When you're ready to travel, make a garment bag and matching tote.

All the designs in this book are for beginning to intermediate-level sewers. Whether you sew them for yourself and your home, or give them as gifts to your family and friends, you'll love the sewing designs in this book.

Dyeing for a Picnic, page 89

Metric Conversion Charts

yards	x	.9144	=	metres (m)
yards	x	91.44	=	centimetres (cm)
inches	x	2.54	=	centimetres (cm)
inches	x	25.40	=	millimetres (mm)
inches	x	.0254	=	metres (m)

centimetres	x	.3937	=	inches
metres	x	1.0936	=	yards

Standard Equivalents

⅛ inch	=	3.20 mm	=	0.32 cm
¼ inch	=	6.35 mm	=	0.635 cm
⅜ inch	=	9.50 mm	=	0.95 cm
½ inch	=	12.70 mm	=	1.27 cm
⅝ inch	=	15.90 mm	=	1.59 cm
¾ inch	=	19.10 mm	=	1.91 cm
⅞ inch	=	22.20 mm	=	2.22 cm
1 inch	=	25.40 mm	=	2.54 cm
⅛ yard	=	11.43 cm	=	0.11 m
¼ yard	=	22.86 cm	=	0.23 m
⅜ yard	=	34.29 cm	=	0.34 m
½ yard	=	45.72 cm	=	0.46 m
⅝ yard	=	57.15 cm	=	0.57 m
¾ yard	=	68.58 cm	=	0.69 m
⅞ yard	=	80.00 cm	=	0.80 m
1 yard	=	91.44 cm	=	0.91 m
1⅛ yard	=	102.87 cm	=	1.03 m
1¼ yard	=	114.30 cm	=	1.14 m
1⅜ yard	=	125.73 cm	=	1.26 m
1½ yard	=	137.16 cm	=	1.37 m
1⅝ yard	=	148.59 cm	=	1.49 m
1¾ yard	=	160.02 cm	=	1.60 m
1⅞ yard	=	171.44 cm	=	1.71 m
2 yards	=	182.88 cm	=	1.83 m

2⅛ yards	=	194.31 cm	=	1.94 m
2¼ yards	=	205.74 cm	=	2.06 m
2⅜ yards	=	217.17 cm	=	2.17 m
2½ yards	=	228.60 cm	=	2.29 m
2⅝ yards	=	240.03 cm	=	2.40 m
2¾ yards	=	251.46 cm	=	2.51 m
2⅞ yards	=	262.88 cm	=	2.63 m
3 yards	=	274.32 cm	=	2.74 m
3⅛ yards	=	285.75 cm	=	2.86 m
3¼ yards	=	297.18 cm	=	2.97 m
3⅜ yards	=	308.61 cm	=	3.09 m
3½ yards	=	320.04 cm	=	3.20 m
3⅝ yards	=	331.47 cm	=	3.31 m
3¾ yards	=	342.90 cm	=	3.43 m
3⅞ yards	=	354.32 cm	=	3.54 m
4 yards	=	365.76 cm	=	3.66 m
4⅛ yards	=	377.19 cm	=	3.77 m
4¼ yards	=	388.62 cm	=	3.89 m
4⅜ yards	=	400.05 cm	=	4.00 m
4½ yards	=	411.48 cm	=	4.11 m
4⅝ yards	=	422.91 cm	=	4.23 m
4¾ yards	=	434.34 cm	=	4.34 m
4⅞ yards	=	445.76 cm	=	4.46 m
5 yards	=	457.20 cm	=	4.57 m

GENERAL INSTRUCTIONS

Basic Sewing Supplies & Equipment

- Sewing machine and matching thread
- Serger, if desired
- Scissors of various sizes, including pinking shears
- Rotary cutter(s), mats and straightedges
- Pattern-tracing paper or cloth
- Pressing tools such as sleeve rolls and June Tailor boards
- Pressing equipment, including ironing board and iron; press cloths
- Straight pins and pincushion
- Measuring tools
- Marking pens (either air- or water-soluble) or tailor's chalk
- Spray adhesive (temporary)
- Hand-sewing needles and thimble
- Point turners

Making Bias Strips

Fold fabric on the diagonal (Figure 1) so the lengthwise grain (selvage edge) is parallel to the crosswise grain (cut edge). Pin and press fabric along the fold. Open fold. Measuring from the pressed line, mark points parallel to the pressed line, spacing them the exact cutting width for desired bias width. For the length of each strip, mark a line diagonal to the lengthwise grain of the fabric at each point (Figure 2) to equal the approximate cutting length indicated in the pillow instructions. Cut bias strips.

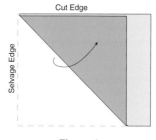

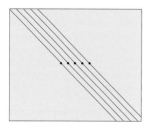

| Figure 1 | Figure 2 |

With right sides facing, align the short ends of two strips at right angles (an L shape). Stitch a narrow seam along the diagonal edge. Press the seam open. Continue to join short ends together until you have a continuous loop of bias strips joined together at the short ends in a length equal to the pattern instructions.

Fusible Tips

When tracing appliqué shapes on the paper side of the fusible web, be sure to allow space between shapes so that each shape is cut loosely around the tracing lines. Cut out each paper shape approximately ¼ inch larger than your drawing lines and iron them onto the wrong side of fabric.

Be sure to follow manufacturer's directions for fusing time, remembering to always test your fusible web on a scrap piece of fabric.

Lay out each appliqué piece before fusing to help you visualize your design. Use a layout that starts at the back and work your way forward. Layering appliqués will give your project depth.

How to Appliqué

To ensure success in your appliqué motifs with no wrinkling or puckering, be sure to provide your fabrics with enough stabilizers in the form of interfacing and fusible web. It is best to support both the base fabric and appliqué motif with a nonwoven fusible interfacing; then adhere the motif to the base fabric with fusible web before you begin to stitch.

For pattern templates, using paper and pencil, individually trace each pattern piece onto cardboard or poster board. Cut out each template. These can be used to draw multiple designs.

A pattern frame will help to position the appliqué motifs each time the design is repeated. Transfer the frame outline and the design within the frame onto tracing paper. Cut this out along the frame line.

For each appliqué motif, cut squares of fabric in the appropriate colour and matching size squares of lightweight, fusible interfacing and fusible web. Following the instructions provided by the manufacturers of these products, fuse the interfacing to the wrong side of the fabric; then fuse the web to the interfacing. When the three layers are adhered and have cooled, using the templates, draw the shape needed onto the wrong side of the stabilized fabric. Cut out the appliqué.

To fuse the appliqué, with right side facing up, position motifs as desired on the right side of the base fabric. Using the frame as a guide and looking through its transparency, place it over the fabric motifs and adjust their position. The edge of the frame should surround entire motif appliqués.

On the wrong side of the base fabric, position the interfacing, sticky side down, in alignment with the motif design on the opposite side. HINT: Hold the fabric up to the light to locate the position of the motif. Fuse the interfacing in place. With interfacing supporting the base and appliqué fabric plus fusible web holding it all in place, you are now free to stitch without fear of puckering.

Set the sewing machine for a zigzag stitch. This will be a medium to wide stitch width and a very short stitch length. Attach a zigzag presser foot, and you might consider changing the top tension dial to a buttonhole setting. Practice this satin stitch on a scrap of fabric.

When stitching the motif in place, use a satin stitch and allow the left-hand swing of the needle to catch the motif and the right hand swing of the needle to enter the base fabric next to the edge of the motif. A medium steady speed is best for satin stitching.

Applying Binding

Lining up the raw edges, place the binding on the top of the quilt and begin sewing (again using the walking foot) approximately 6 inches from the beginning of the binding strip. Stop sewing ¼ inch from the first corner, leave the needle in the quilt,

turn and sew diagonally to the corner as shown in Figure 3.

Figure 3

Fold the binding at a 45-degree angle up and away from the quilt as shown in Figure 4 and back down even with the raw edge of the next side of the quilt. Starting at the top raw edge of the quilt, begin sewing the next side as shown in Figure 5. Repeat at the next three corners.

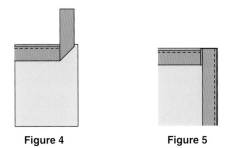

Figure 4   Figure 5

As you approach the beginning of the binding strip, stop stitching and overlap the binding ends ½ inch; trim. Join the two ends with a ¼-inch seam allowance and press the seam open. Reposition the joined binding along the edge of the quilt and resume stitching to the beginning.

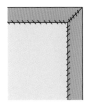

Figure 6

To finish, bring the folded edge of the binding over the raw edges and blind-stitch the binding in place over the machine-stitching line on the back side. Hand-miter the corners on the back as shown in Figure 6. ◆

Bee-Dazzled Summer

Do be a do bee and sew this "bee-dazzled" table runner. It will draw in your guests like bees to honey, and you'll be sure to create a buzz at your next summer occasion.

DESIGN BY CAROLYN S. VAGTS

Skill Level
Beginner

Finished Size
44½ x 18 inches

Materials
- 45-inch-wide fabric:
    1 yard cream dot for background, outer border, backing and binding
    ⅛ yard dark green batik for accent border
    ⅓ yard cream mottled for diamond backgrounds
- ½ yard thin batting
- Fabric scraps for appliqué*:
    light green batik
    dark green batik
    brown batik
    gold batik
    yellow batik
    black solid
- Fusible web
- Black #8 pearl cotton
- Basic sewing supplies and equipment

*Scraps of accent border fabric were used for dark green on model project.

Cutting
From fabric for background, outer border and binding:
- Cut one 14½-inch square; subcut square into quarters diagonally making four triangles.
- Cut four 2½-inch strips the width of the fabric for outer border.
- Cut three 2-inch strips the width of the fabric for binding.

Note: Backing will be cut later.

From fabric for accent border:
- Cut three 1-inch strips the width of the fabric.

From diamond background fabric:
- Cut three 9½-inch squares.

From fabric scraps for appliqué:
- Apply fusible web to the backs of scraps. Using patterns provided, cut sunflower petals, sunflower centre, extra petals, leaves and ½ x 7-inch strips for stems to make two sunflowers; cut bee body from yellow and bee stripes, head and wings from black to make one bee.

Note: Stems can be made using a wide satin stitch, if preferred.

Assembly

Note: *Use ¼-inch-wide seam allowances unless otherwise stated.*

1. Sew one quarter-square triangle to one 9½-inch square (Figure 1). Make two units.

Figure 1

2. Sew a quarter-square triangle to each side of the remaining 9½-inch square (Figure 2). Make one unit. Press.

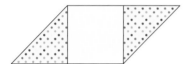

Figure 2

3. Sew units from steps 1 and 2 together (Figure 3). Press.

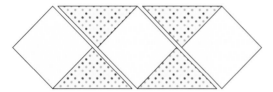

Figure 3

4. Sew the 1-inch-wide accent border to each of the long sides, leaving extra length to trim to maintain shape before adding the two end pieces of accent border. Press. Sew accent border to ends, trimming in same manner. Press.

5. Sew outer border strips to long sides and then to end points in same manner as accent border (Figure 4). Press.

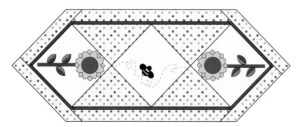

Figure 4

6. Referring to photo, arrange sunflowers and bee in diamond triangles and fuse in place. ***Note:*** *Slip extra petals behind sunflower petals before fusing.*

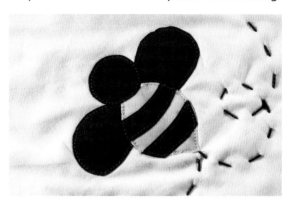

7. Cut backing to fit runner. Sandwich batting between runner and backing. Stitch around edges of appliqué and stitch-in-the-ditch to quilt.

8. Using ⅝-inch seam allowance (and trimming seam to ⅜ inch), bind edges of runner with 2-inch-wide strips.

9. Make running stitch with black pearl cotton to create bee trail. ✦

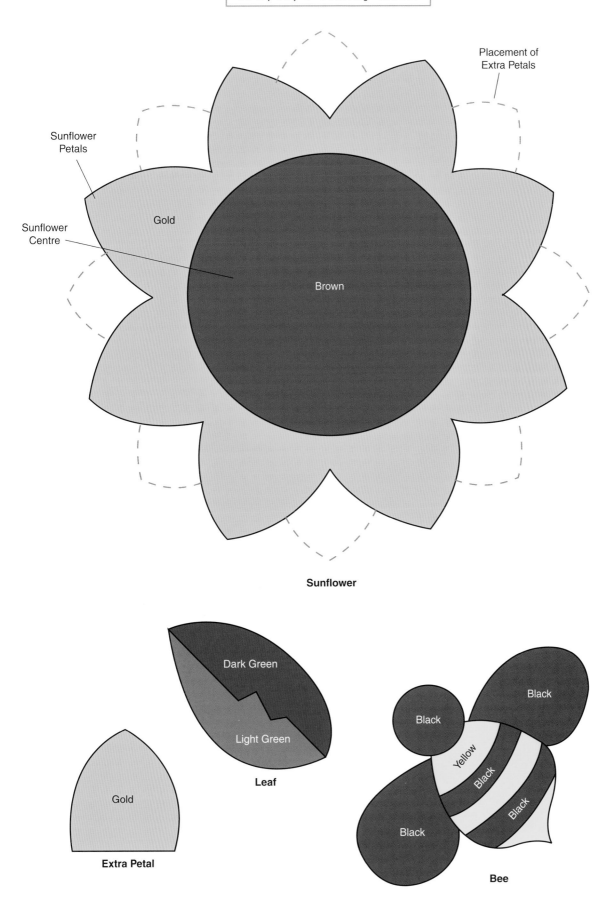

Placement of
Extra Petals

Sunflower
Petals

Gold

Sunflower
Centre

Brown

Sunflower

Dark Green

Light Green

Leaf

Gold

Extra Petal

Black

Black

Yellow

Black

Black

Black

Bee

Knot-ical & Nice

Wake up to nautical appeal with these simple placemats with grommets and cable cord.

DESIGNS BY JANIS BULLIS

Skill Level
Beginner

Finished Sizes
Placemat: 12 x 18 inches
Optional Napkin: 16 x 16 inches

Materials for One Placemat & Napkin
- 44/45-inch-wide cotton fabric:
    ½ yard print for placemat centre (and optional matching print napkin)
    ½ yard coordinating tone-on-tone print for borders and backing
- ½ yard 44-inch-wide lightweight fusible interfacing
- Grommet application tool
- 32 (¼-inch-diameter) silver grommets
- 2¼ yards ³⁄₁₆-inch-diameter cotton cable cord
- Basic sewing supplies and equipment

Cutting
From the print for placemat centre:
- Cut one 9 x 15-inch rectangle.
- Optional: Cut one 17-inch square for napkin.

From border/backing fabric:
- Cut one 13 x 19-inch rectangle for placemat backing.
- Cut two 3 x 14-inch strips for short borders.
- Cut two 3 x 20-inch strips for long borders.

From the fusible interfacing:
- Cut one 9 x 15-inch rectangle.

- Cut two each 3 x 14-inch and 3 x 20-inch strips for borders.

Assembly
Note: *Use ½-inch-wide seam allowances unless otherwise directed.*

1. Fuse interfacing to the wrong side of the 9 x 15-inch centre rectangle and the 3-inch-wide border strips.

2. On the wrong side of the centre panel, mark the seam lines at all four corners. With right sides together and long cut edges even, centre and pin one long band to one long edge of the centre panel. With the centre panel on top, stitch from seam-line to seam-line intersection. Begin and end with backstitching (Figure 1).

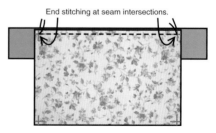

Figure 1

3. Add the remaining border strips in the same manner.

4. Trim the seams to ¼ inch wide and finger-press toward the placemat centre.

5. To mitre each corner, fold the mat diagonally with the long edges of the adjacent borders even. Draw a 45-degree-angle stitching line from the seam intersection to the outer edge; stitch on the

line and trim the excess, leaving a ¼-inch-wide seam allowance (Figure 2).

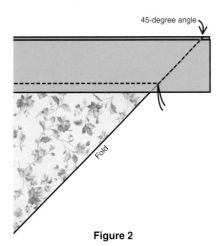

45-degree angle

Fold

Figure 2

6. After mitring all four corners in this manner, press the border seam allowances toward the outer edges of the completed placemat front.

7. With right sides together, pin together placemat front and 13 x 19-inch rectangle for placemat backing; stitch ½ inch from raw edges, leaving a 6-inch-long opening in one long edge for turning. Backstitch at the beginning and end of the seam. Clip the corners, trim the seam

allowances to ¼ inch and turn the placemat right side out; press, turning in the opening edges. Slipstitch the edges together.

8. Mark the grommet placements along all edges as shown in Figure 3. Apply the grommets through all layers following the package directions.

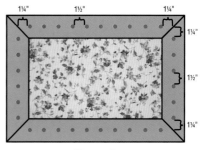

1¼"   1½"   1¼"

1¼"

1½"

1¼"

Figure 3

9. Lace cord through the grommets, tying a knot at each corner. To finish cord ends on the underside, cut the cord ends so they butt and whipstitch together. Wrap the ends with a scrap of fabric or ribbon, and glue in place with permanent fabric adhesive.

10. To finish the napkin square, turn under and press a narrow hem all around, and then topstitch or use your serger to finish the edges with a rolled edge. ✦

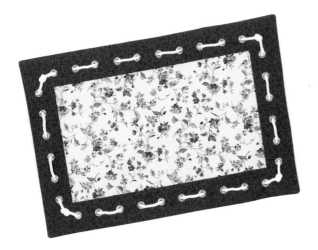

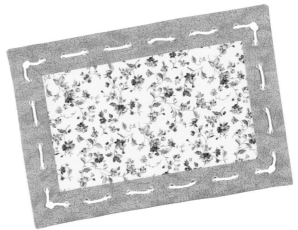

Ribbons Galore

Nothing says extravagant like these beautifully beribboned placemats, napkins and rings. Easy to sew, simply purchase ribbons for enhancement and enjoy.

DESIGNS BY CAROL ZENTGRAF

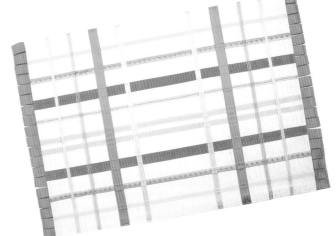

Skill Level
Beginner

Finished Sizes
Placemat: 19½ x 13 inches
Napkin: 18 x 18 inches
Napkin Ring: Approximately 17 inches long

Materials for One Placemat
- ½ yard 45-inch-wide white cotton fabric
- ½ yard heavyweight fusible interfacing
- Ribbons:
    8 yards total assorted ¼–¾-inch-wide for top
    2¾ yards ¾-inch-wide for edges
- Self-adhesive double-sided basting tape
- Clear gridded quilter's ruler
- Invisible thread
- Basic sewing supplies and equipment

Cutting
From white cotton fabric:
• Cut two 19 x 14-inch rectangles.

From interfacing:
• Cut two 19 x 14-inch rectangles.

Assembly
1. Follow manufacturer's directions to fuse interfacing to the wrong side of the cotton-fabric rectangles.
2. Cut assorted-width ribbons into eight 14-inch lengths for vertical strips and nine 19-inch lengths for horizontal strips. Referring to photo for placement, arrange ribbons on right side of one cotton rectangle, keeping top and bottom horizontal ribbons 1½ inches from edges.
3. Centre and adhere a strip of double-sided basting tape to the wrong side of each ribbon length. Using the clear ruler to keep strips straight and parallel to the edges, adhere horizontal strips first and then the vertical strips.
4. With white all-purpose thread in the bobbin and invisible thread in the needle, stitch the centre of each narrow ribbon strip in place. For each wider-ribbon strip, stitch along both edges.
5. From ¾-inch-wide ribbon for edges, cut 38 lengths each 2½ inches long. On the right side of

the ribbon-embellished rectangle, place a piece of basting tape along each short edge, ¼ inch from the edge. Adhere 2½-inch-long ribbons evenly spaced across ends of placemat, with ribbon end overlapping placemat edge ¼ inch. Place a second layer of basting tape across each short edge of the placemat as before, over ribbon ends; then fold the ribbon strips in half with ends even (Figure 1).

Figure 1

6. Press under top and bottom edges of each placemat rectangle ½ inch. Use basting tape to adhere rectangles together with right sides out and edges even. Edge-stitch panels together using invisible thread.

Napkin

Materials for One Napkin
- 19-inch square cotton fabric in desired colour
- 2¼ yards ¼-inch-wide ribbon
- Rayon machine-embroidery thread
- Basic sewing supplies and equipment

Assembly
1. Press under edges of fabric ¼ inch. Press under ¼ inch again and edge-stitch hem in place using matching all-purpose thread.
2. With rayon machine-embroidery thread and a long, narrow zigzag stitch, stitch ribbon around edges of napkin over edge stitching.

Napkin Ring

Materials for One Napkin Ring
- ½ yard 1½-inch-wide sheer ribbon
- 1½-inch-diameter sequin flower
- Permanent fabric adhesive
- Seam sealant

Assembly
1. Tie a knot in the centre of the ribbon.
2. Glue centre back of flower to knot using permanent fabric adhesive.
3. Apply seam sealant to cut ends of ribbon. Let dry. ◆

Twisted Basket & Quilted Table Topper

Nothing says unique better than this pretty round bowl resting on top of a matching quilted table topper.

DESIGNS BY SUSAN BREIER

Skill Level
Intermediate

Finished Sizes
Basket: 7-inch diameter at base, 11½-inch diameter at top, 4½ inches tall
Table Topper: 21½ inches square

Materials
- 65 feet ³⁄₁₆-inch flexible clothesline with no hard-centre core
- 8 different-colour fat quarters of cotton fabric for basket strips (3 colours are also used for borders and binding of table topper)
- ⅔ yard 45-inch-wide cotton fabric for front centre panel and four cornerstones of table topper and strips for basket
- ⅞ yard 45-inch-wide coordinating piece of cotton fabric for table topper backing
- 25 x 25-inch square low-loft batting
- 20 (¾-inch) flat buttons
- New 80 or 90 universal machine needles
- Variety of hand-sewing needles
- 50 (1-inch) brass safety pins or 50 straight pins
- 2 acid-free glue sticks
- Masking tape or coloured tape
- Needle-nose pliers
- Bamboo stick or stiletto
- Single-stitch foot and throat plate for table topper

- Zigzag foot or open appliqué foot and zigzag throat plate for basket
- Acrylic extension table or equivalent (to extend level sewing surface)
- Basic sewing supplies and equipment

Cutting
Note: Use rotary cutter, mat and ruler.
From fabric for centre panel and cornerstones:
- Cut one 16 x 16-inch square for centre panel.
- Cut four 3½-inch squares for cornerstones.

From fabric for backing:
- Cut one 25 x 25-inch square for backing.

From fat quarters for borders, binding and basket:
- Cut four 1½ x 18-inch strips from each of three different-colour prints for table topper borders.
- Cut 2¼-inch-wide strips on the bias to total 52 inches when joined for binding. *Note: Use same colour as selected for border strip next to centre panel.*
- After other pieces have been cut, begin rotary-cutting ½- to ¾-inch-wide strips for the basket. *Note: Cut only a few strips at a time to conserve fabric and prevent fraying from handling.*

Table Topper Assembly
Note: Use a ¼-inch-wide seam allowance unless otherwise stated.

1. Place the 12 border strips in four groups of three each. Straight-stitch together each group of border strips. Press seams toward what will be the outer edge.

2. Trim two of the four assembled borders to 16 inches. Straight-stitch these pieces to two opposite sides of the 16-inch centre panel (Figure 1). Press seams.

Figure 1

3. Trim remaining assembled borders to 16½ inches long. Sew a cornerstone to each end of each remaining assembled borders. Press seams. Straight-stitch assembled pieces to remaining sides of centre panel unit (Figure 2). Press seams. Trim edges even.

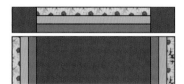

Figure 2

4. With wrong side up, tape backing piece tautly on a flat, even work surface. Centre the 25 x 25-inch square of batting over backing, then centre the pieced top over the batting with right side up. Using safety pins or straight pins, pin together layers, beginning in centre and working outward.

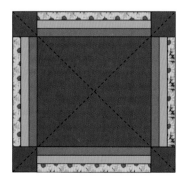

Figure 3

5. Remove tape. Beginning at the outer edge of one cornerstone, straight-stitch across the cornerstone diagonally to the opposite corner. Stitch diagonally across the cornerstone between opposite corners (Figure 3).

6. Make a 1-inch-wide paper guide to help stitch a total of seven straight lines centred diagonally across the centre panel in both directions (Figure 4).

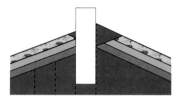

Figure 4

7. Stitch in the ditch at border and cornerstone seams, working diagonal lines on each cornerstone as you come to it.

8. Machine-baste ⅛ inch around outer edge of assembled centre panel. Trim off excess batting and backing.

9. Bind edges with 2¼-inch-wide bias strips using a ⅝-inch-wide seam allowance and trimming seam to ⅜ inch.

10. Hand-stitch a button in the centre of each cornerstone.

Basket Assembly

Note: *Use either zigzag foot or an open appliqué foot and zigzag bed.*

1. Apply glue to 1 inch of both the wrong side of the fabric strip and the end of the clothesline. Wrap approximately 4 inches of line with fabric; pin in place to hold. Beginning at the end, straight-stitch a basting line for 2 inches (Figure 5). Remove from the machine and cut threads. Continue wrapping fabric around line, occasionally using a dab of glue.

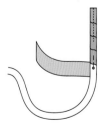

Figure 5

2. Tightly wrap coil so it is about 1 inch in diameter. *Note: Use the machine bed to help maintain that shape.* Straight-stitch an "X" over the coil for easier zigzagging later (Figure 6). Remove from machine and cut threads.

Figure 6

3. Using a predetermined stitch setting (see **Consistent Stitches** tip in Sewing Tips sidebar, page 24) zigzag edges of line together, starting at beginning of the coil (Figure 7). *Notes: Use the needle-down option to hold the line under the presser foot and free both hands. You will need to reposition the coil often because of stitching in a small area. A bamboo stick or stiletto will help twirl the coil under the needle.* Continue wrapping and zigzagging until the coiled base is 1⅞ inches in diameter.

Figure 7

4. Choose a different-colour fabric strip. Overlap the end of the previous fabric and pin together. Continue wrapping and stitching as before.

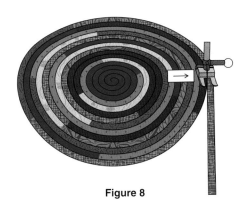

Figure 8

5. Add new colours of staggered lengths of fabric to achieve a patchwork affect. When base reaches a diameter of 7 inches, prepare to begin shaping the sides. Place a piece of tape on the coil to the left of the needle to mark where to change hand positions (Figure 8).

6. At the tape marker, with the needle down, lift the base halfway between the machine bed and the flat side of the needle arm (Figure 9). Zigzag one row until you again meet the marker. Stop with the needle down.

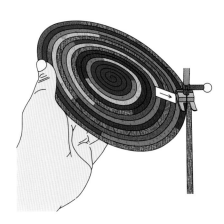

Figure 9

7. Change hand position so base touches the side of the needle arm (Figure 10). Continue stitching until the side measures 2 inches at the marker.

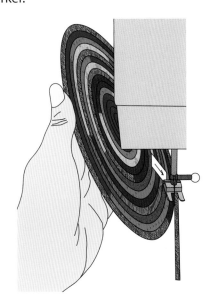

Figure 10

8. At this point, allow the side of the basket to fall onto the extension table as you sew. The top of the basket will widen and create V-shaped sides. Continue in this position until the side measures 4 inches at the marker (Figure 11).

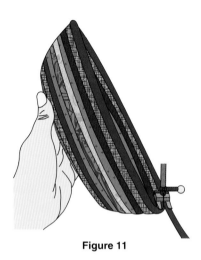

Figure 11

9. Wrap and zigzag three continuous rows using a focal colour.

10. To finish off the end, apply glue to the fabric only and wrap line more firmly so the end tapers to just-wrapped fabric. Cut off remaining fabric and zigzag this area to finish the rim of the basket. *Note: Use a bamboo stick or stiletto to guide this end of line tightly to the adjacent row. If end is bumpy, push straight pins into the rim and leave in place until glue dries.*

11. To help prevent the top from fraying and to strengthen the project, secure the top edge by zigzagging around it once on the fabric and one more time just off the rim.

12. Embellish the top edge of the basket with 16 (¾-inch) buttons sewn evenly spaced around the top three rows. *Note: Needle-nose pliers will help pull the needle through the thickness.* Cut off fraying threads. ◆

Sewing Tips

A Must: Clean and oil machine before beginning. Insert a new needle.

Preparing Fabric: Always wash, machine dry and iron fabric before beginning project.

Hint: When wrapping, glue and pin at the beginning and the end of each strip to help hold it in place until the area has been sewn. Don't wrap more than a yard of line at a time. Always sew whatever you have glued. Dried glue may make your stitches irregular.

Keeping Track of the Tail: The tail is the wrapped line ready to be sewn. Keep the tail moving through the area that forms the arch or very centre of your machine bed. Check this often as it is common to reverse the coil.

Consistent Stitches: Using zigzag attachments, make several wrapped sample lines to test which setting for zigzag is best. The stitches should touch adjacent lines evenly without entering the very centre of the lines. Ideally the tops of the zigzags are ⅛ inch apart. Write the correct setting on tape and place it on the front of your machine as a reminder.

Fixing Mistakes: Occasionally, after wrapping and stitching, a portion of the line may show through. Use a permanent marker to colour in a very small area. If you need to cover a larger area, cut a scrap of the same-colour fabric, and glue and stitch it in place. Check for areas where stitches are off. Go back to that area and restitch. No one will ever know!

Joining Lines: It is easy to join lines together. Glue and overlap the unwrapped lines by ½ inch. Hold the area together. Wind an 18-inch piece of thread tightly around the joined area. Finger-press to decrease bulk and wrap tightly with fabric; zigzag while glue is wet.

Sweet as Chocolate

Sew this pretty pink and brown table topper to create a passion-filled and chocolate-flavoured Valentine's Day.

DESIGN BY CAROLYN S. VAGTS

Skill Level
Intermediate

Finished Size
24 x 24 inches

Materials
- 45-inch-wide fabric:
    ⅓ yard light pink for squares in centre
    ⅓ yard medium pink for squares in centre
    1½ yards dark pink for border and binding
    ¼ yard brown batik for flange and appliqués
    scraps fuchsia batik for heart appliqués
- 1 yard fusible web
- Batting to size
- Basic sewing supplies and equipment

Cutting
From light pink fabric:
- Cut three 2½-inch strips the width of the fabric; subcut strips into 41 (2½-inch) squares for centre.

From medium pink fabric:
- Cut three 2½-inch strips the width of the fabric; subcut strips into 40 (2½-inch) squares for centre.

From dark pink fabric:
Note: Backing will be cut later.
- Cut three 3½-inch strips the width of the fabric for border.

- Cut four 2½-inch strips the width of the fabric for binding.

From brown batik fabric:
- Cut two 1¼-inch strips the width of the fabric; subcut strips into four 20-inch lengths.
- Apply fusible web to scraps. Cut four large hearts and four medium hearts.

From scraps of fuchsia batik:
- Apply fusible web. Cut four scallop hearts, four medium hearts and eight small hearts.

Assembly
1. Sew one 2½-inch medium pink square between two 2½-inch light pink squares (Figure 1). Repeat to make 14 units.

Figure 1   Figure 2

2. Sew one 2½-inch light pink square between two 2½-inch medium pink squares (Figure 2). Repeat to make 13 units.

3. Using units from steps 1 and 2, make a total of nine blocks as shown in Figures 3A and 3B: five blocks with light pink corners and four blocks with medium pink corners.

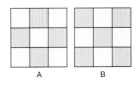

A   B

Figure 3

4. Referring to Figure 4 for placement, sew blocks together to make an 18½-inch square.

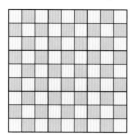

Figure 4

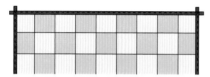

Figure 5

5. Press flange strips in half with right sides out. With raw edges even, sew a flange to the top and bottom of the 18½-inch square and then to each side. ***Note:*** *Fold flange on a 45-degree angle at both corners as you add the side pieces to give the appearance of mitred corners (Figure 5).*

6. Sew border pieces to the top and bottom of the unit and then to the sides (Figure 6).

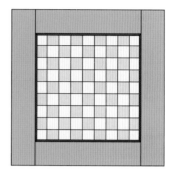

Figure 6

7. Referring to photo for placement, fuse appliqués in place. Topstitch close to edges of each appliqué piece.

8. Cut backing to fit runner. Sandwich batting between runner and backing. Stitch around edges of appliqué and stitch-in-the-ditch to quilt.

9. Using ⅝-inch seam allowance (and trimming seam to ⅜ inch), bind edges of runner with 2½-inch-wide strips. ◆

Large Scallop Heart

Large Heart

Medium Heart

Small Heart

Sunny Day Topper

Brighten any day with this summery-looking table topper.

DESIGN BY CONNIE KAUFFMAN

Skill Level
Beginner

Finished Size
32 x 16 inches

Materials
- 1 fat quarter each yellow, blue, green and multicoloured prints
- Backing 38 x 22 inches
- Batting 38 x 22 inches
- Quilting thread
- Basic sewing supplies and equipment

Cutting
- Cut (22) 2⅞ x 2⅞-inch A squares yellow print.
- Cut one 4⅛ x 4⅛-inch square each yellow (F) and blue (G) prints; cut each square on both diagonals to make four each F and G triangles.
- Cut (28) 2⅞ x 2⅞-inch B squares blue print.
- Cut (20) 2⅞ x 2⅞-inch C squares green print.
- Cut (10) 2⅞ x 2⅞-inch D squares multicoloured print.
- Cut seven 5¼ x 5¼-inch squares multicoloured print; cut each square on both diagonals to make 28 E triangles.

Completing the Topper
1. Cut all A, B, C and D squares in half on one diagonal to make triangles.
2. Join triangles on the diagonals as shown in Figure 1 to make triangle units; press seams toward darker fabric.

Figure 1

3. Sew A, B, C and D triangles to E to make rectangle units as shown in Figure 2; press seams away from E.

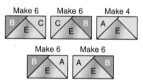

Figure 2

4. Join the triangle units to make four-unit sections as shown in Figure 3; press seams in one direction.

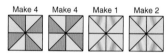

Figure 3

5. Join the rectangle units to make square units as shown in Figure 4; press seams in one direction.

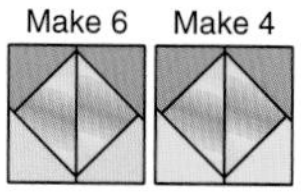

Figure 4

6. Arrange the four-unit sections with the square units in rows with the remaining rectangle and triangle units, and the F and G triangles referring to Figure 5; press seams in one direction.

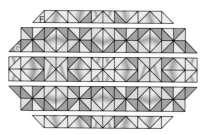

Figure 5

7. Trim off the B-C end units even with the angles of F and G as shown in Figure 6 to complete the top.

Figure 6

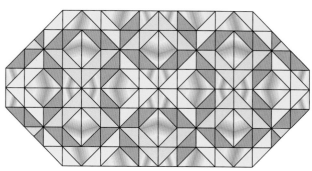

Sunny Day Topper
Placement Diagram
32" x 16"

8. Place the batting and backing right side up and topper right side down.
9. Stitch all around outside edge of topper, leaving a 3-inch opening on one side. Trim batting and backing even with the topper edge.
10. Turn topper right side out through the opening; press flat.
11. Press opening edges inside ¼ inch; hand-stitch opening closed.
12. Quilt as desired by hand or machine to finish. ◆

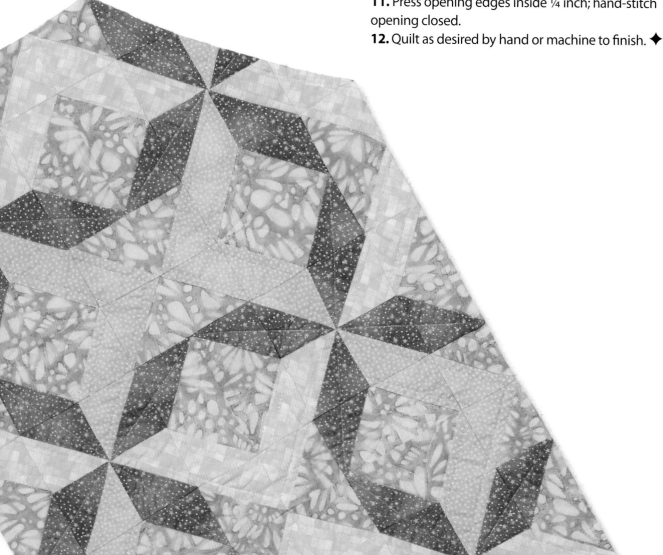

Wintry Pines

Use wool felt to create this table runner reminiscent of the penny rugs popularized during the mid-1800s. It's the perfect table accent for the snowy days of winter.

DESIGNS BY PAMELA J. CECIL

Skill Level
Beginner

Finished Sizes
Runner: 13 x 40 inches
Coaster: 4½ inches square

Materials
- 1¼ yards light tan felt
- ¼ yard green felt
- ¼ yard gold felt
- 9 x 12-inch piece (or scraps) brown felt
- 9 x 12-inch piece (or scraps) rust felt
- 4 skeins brown 6-strand embroidery floss
- 1 skein each green, rust and gold 6-strand embroidery floss
- Lightweight paper-backed fusible web
- Chenille/candlewicking needle
- Basic sewing supplies and equipment

Instructions
1. Cut two 15 x 36-inch pieces for the runner from the light tan felt.
2. Trace the tab template on page 155 onto template plastic or poster board and cut out. Hold the tab pattern in place on a double layer of light tan felt and cut 12 double-layer tabs. Pin each pair of tabs together to keep them in matched pairs during the runner construction.

3. Trace the appliqué templates on page 155 onto the paper side of the fusible web, leaving at least ¼ inch of space between motifs. Trace the required number of each one as directed on the templates.
4. Cut out the shapes with a ⅛-inch-wide margin all around. Apply to felt of the appropriate colour as given on the template. Cut out the shapes on the drawn lines and remove the paper backing from each one.
5. Working on a large, flat surface, centre a large rust felt "penny" on one of the tan felt rectangles. Centre a gold penny on top of it. Referring to Figure 1, arrange the stems, leaves, and hearts with gold pennies around the centre circle. When satisfied with the arrangement, place a press cloth over the pieces and fuse in place following the manufacturer's directions.

Figure 1

6. Referring to Figure 2, position the lower end of a tree trunk 1 inch above each short end of the tan felt rectangle. Make sure the piece is

Figure 2

centred from side to side and then fuse in place. Position the tree branches on each side of each trunk and a star above each one and fuse in place.

7. Referring to Figure 3, centre a small gold penny on top of each remaining large rust penny. Place each stack on a pair of tabs about ½ inch from the lower edge. Fuse in place.

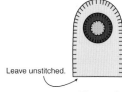

Leave unstitched.

Figure 3

8. Use 3 strands of embroidery floss for all stitching. Blanket-stitch around the appliqué edges using the following thread colours: brown for leaves and branches; green for tree trunks and stems; gold for hearts and large pennies; rust for stars and small pennies. ***Note:*** *When sewing the pennies in place on the tabs, set the lower tab of the pair aside while you stitch the pennies to the upper tab. Then pin the lower tab to its mate to keep them together.*

9. Blanket-stitch around the curved edges of the tabs using brown embroidery floss (Figure 3).

10. Refer to Figure 4 for Steps 10 and 11. With the appliquéd runner faceup on a flat surface, arrange six tabs along each short end. Place them right sides together with raw edges even and stitched edges next to each other; pin in place. There should be a ¾-inch-wide allowance at each long edge. Machine-baste the tabs in place.

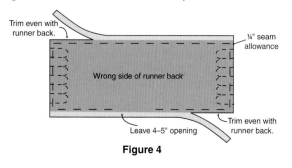

Trim even with runner back.

¼" seam allowance

Wrong side of runner back

Leave 4–5" opening

Trim even with runner back.

Figure 4

11. Pin the runner rectangles together with right sides facing. Stitch ¾ inch from the long raw edges and ¼ inch from the short ends. Leave a 5-inch-long opening in one long side for turning. Trim the seams to ¼ inch at the long edges. Turn the runner right side out and hand-stitch the opening closed.

12. Using the brown floss, blanket-stitch over all edges of the runner, stitching only over the edge of the top layer. Repeat on the back side of the rectangle.

Matching Coasters

1. Cut four double layers of tan felt, each measuring 42 inches square.

2. Using the runner appliqué templates on page 155, trace two hearts, two stars, 16 leaves, two stems and four pennies onto the paper side of the fusible web. Leave at least ¼ inch of space between the pieces. Cut out each shape with a ⅛-inch margin beyond the drawn lines.

3. Apply the fusible web to the appropriate-colour felt for each piece (refer to the photos). Cut out on the traced lines and remove the paper backing.

4. Referring to the photos, position the appliqués on the top piece of each of the four pairs of tan felt and fuse in place following the manufacturer's directions. Use a press cloth to protect the felt.

5. Using 3 strands of embroidery floss, blanket-stitch around the pieces using the following colours: brown for leaves; green for stems; gold for hearts; gold for the rust pennies; and rust for the gold pennies.

6. Use brown embroidery floss to blanket-stitch the coaster layers together around all four edges. ✦

TEMPLATES ON PAGE 155

Autumn Leaves

Colour-blocked panels embellished with simply stitched leaves add up to a seasonal setting for your dining table. Combine fabric textures and fall colours to create this easy-sew ensemble.

DESIGNS BY LYNN WEGLARZ

Skill Level
Beginner

Finished Sizes
Table Runner: 17¾ x 67 inches
Placemat: 11½ x 18 inches
Napkin: 19¼ inches square

Materials for Table Runner
Note: *Look for a variety of textures in the same colour family for your table runner and placemats for a one-of-a-kind look. Refer to the photos and assembly diagrams for placement within the project.*
- 2 yards Fabric A for front and runner backing
- ⅓ yard each Fabrics B, C and G
- ¼ yard each Fabrics D, F, H and J
- ⅜ yard each Fabrics E and I
- 1 package iron-on, tear-away embroidery stabilizer
- Monofilament nylon or polyester thread

Materials for Placemat A
- ⅛ yard each Fabrics A and D
- ⅓ yard Fabric B
- ¼ yard Fabric C
- ½ yard Fabric E for front and backing
- 12½ x 19-inch piece lightweight cotton batting
- Temporary spray adhesive (optional)

Materials for Placemat B
- ⅛ yard each Fabrics A and D
- ¼ yard each Fabrics B and C
- ½ yard Fabric E for front and backing
- 12½ x 19-inch piece lightweight cotton batting
- Temporary spray adhesive (optional)

Materials for One Double-Layer Napkin
- 2 (20-inch squares) cotton print (cut from ⅝ yard 44/45-inch-wide fabric)
- 1 package ½-inch-wide paper-backed fusible web tape
- Rotary cutter, mat and ruler
- Wave blade for rotary cutter
- Iron

Materials for All Projects
- Template plastic
- Decorative metallic or rayon embroidery thread for leaves
- Sewing machine needle for metallic thread
- Basic sewing supplies and equipment

Cutting
Note: *Preshrink all the fabrics and press to remove wrinkles. This is particularly important if you are using different weights, textures and fibre contents as in the projects shown.*

From each fabric, cut the required pieces for the runner or placemat you are making. Refer to the assembly diagrams for fabric identification, colour and placement.

Table Runner
Fabric A: 18¼ x 7¼ inches and 18¼ x 67½ inches for backing
Fabric B: 9⅜ x 11¾ inches
Fabric C: 9⅜ x 11¾ inches
Fabric D: 18¼ x 5¾ inches
Fabric E: 13½ x 15¼ inches
Fabric F: 5¼ x 15¼ inches
Fabric G: 18¼ x 10 inches
Fabric H: 5¼ x 15¼ inches
Fabric I: 13½ x 15¼ inches
Fabric J: 18¼ x 5¼ inches

Placemat A
Fabric A: 2¼ x 12 inches
Fabric B: 10 x 9½ inches
Fabric C: 7¼ x 9½ inches
Fabric D: 16¾ x 1¾ inches
Fabric E: 16¾ x 1¾ inches for the mat and 12 x 18½ inches for the backing

Placemat B
Fabric A: 1½ x 11¼ inches
Fabric B: 7½ x 8¾ inches
Fabric C: 10½ x 8¾ inches
Fabric D: 17½ x 3 inches
Fabric E: 1¼ x 18½ inches for the mat and 12 x 18½ inches for the backing

Table Runner Assembly
Note: *Use ¼-inch-wide seam allowances.*
1. Referring to the assembly diagram, arrange the pieces for the runner in rows. Sew the pieces in each row together and press the seam allowances toward the darker fabric in the row.
2. Sew the rows together and press the seam allowances toward the single-piece strips as shown by the arrows.
3. Following the manufacturer's directions, apply the iron-on stabilizer to the wrong side of one piece where leaves will be stitched.

4. Enlarge the leaf patterns as directed and trace onto template plastic; cut out carefully. Use the chalk marker to draw the desired size leaf design in the section. Refer to the assembly diagram and the photo.

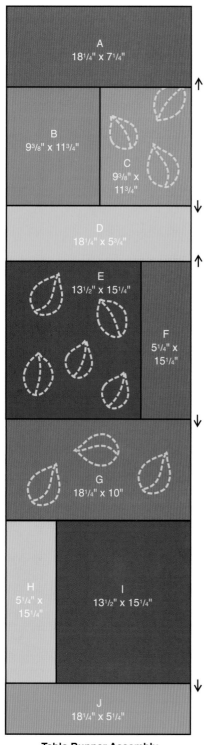

Table Runner Assembly
(With Cutting Dimensions Noted)

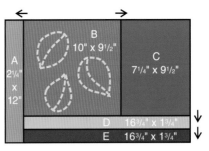

Placemat A Assembly
(With Cutting Dimensions Noted)

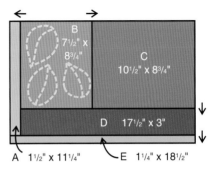

Placemat B Assembly
(With Cutting Dimensions Noted)

5. Refer to Test-Stitch First for balanced stitching. Insert the metallic-thread needle and thread the machine with the decorative metallic thread. Use a straight stitch to stitch along the leaf design lines. Carefully lift and remove the stabilizer.

6. Stabilize, mark and stitch the leaf designs in the remaining sections in the same manner.

7. With right sides together, pin and stitch the pieced runner front to the runner back. Leave a 6-inch-long opening for turning at one of the short ends.

8. Clip the corners and turn right side out. Press, turning in the opening edges and making sure the backing is not visible along the edges on the front of the runner.

9. Slipstitch the opening edges together. Using the decorative thread and metallic needle, topstitch ¼ inch from the outer edges.

10. Thread the machine with the monofilament thread and stitch in the ditch of the piecing seams to tack the pieced front to the runner back.

Placemat Assembly

1. Referring to the assembly diagrams, arrange the pieces for each placemat and sew together in sections. Press the seam allowances as directed by the arrows, and then sew the sections together. Press as directed by the arrows.

2. Centre and smooth the pieced placemat in place on top of the batting. Pin in place (or apply temporary spray adhesive to one side of the batting before smoothing the placemat in place). Machine-baste a scant ¼ inch from the placemat raw edges and trim the excess batting even with the placemat edges.

3. Trace the leaf patterns onto template plastic and cut out carefully. Position the shapes in the panels (see diagrams and photos) and trace

around them using the chalk marker. Stitch as directed in step 5 for the table runner.

4. With right sides facing and raw edges even, stitch each placemat to its backing piece. Leave an opening in one edge. Trim the batting ⅛ inch from the stitching. Clip the corners and turn the placemat right side out. Press, turning in the opening edges. Slipstitch the opening edges together.

5. Topstitch ¼ inch from the outer edges using decorative thread and the metallic needle.

6. With monofilament thread in the needle, stitch in the ditch of the piecing seams to tack the front to the backing and batting.

Double-Layer Napkin Assembly

1. Following the manufacturer's directions, apply strips of paper-backed fusible tape around the outer edge on the wrong side of one of the two squares for each napkin. Make sure that the tape extends all the way to the corners.

2. Remove the paper backing and position the second square in place with wrong sides together. For best results, position the squares so the crosswise and lengthwise grains are in opposing directions. Fuse together following the manufacturer's directions.

3. Place the napkin on the rotary cutting mat and use the decorative blade in the cutter to trim away ¼ inch along each edge of the napkin.

4. *Optional:* Fold the napkins to create a front pocket and tuck sprigs of artificial fall foliage in each one. ✦

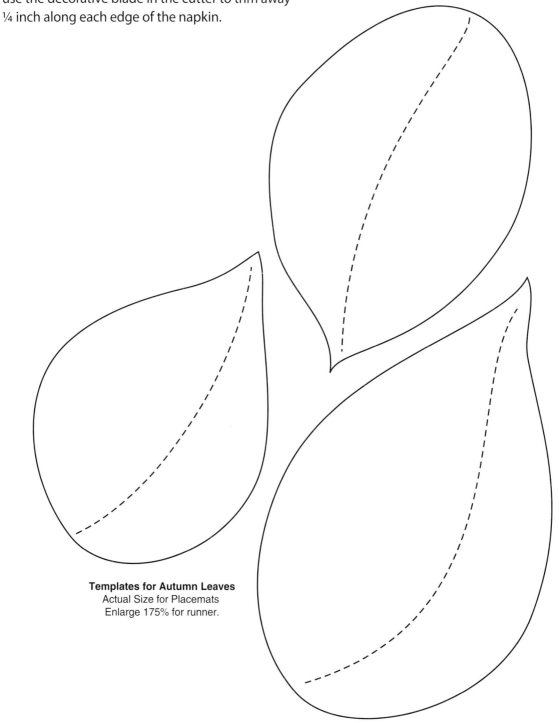

Templates for Autumn Leaves
Actual Size for Placemats
Enlarge 175% for runner.

Nautical & Nice Crib Set

A fleet of bright boats sets sail with a school of colourful fish in this easy-to-stitch baby set.

DESIGNS BY JANE SCHENCK

Skill Level
Intermediate

Finished Sizes
Quilt: 35 x 46½ inches
Bumper Pad: Approximately 9 x 161 inches
Wall Organizer: 14 x 16½ inches
Diaper Stacker: 14 x 26 inches, excluding hanger

Materials
- Purchased pattern for diaper stacker, wall organizer and bumper pad
- 44/45-inch-wide cotton fabric 4 yards multicoloured stripe for quilt, diaper stacker and bumper pad
    - 3½ yards blue print for fish block backgrounds, quilt backing and binding, wall organizer and diaper stacker
    - 1¾ yards blue tone-on-tone print for background in Sailboat blocks
    - ⅝ yard yellow tone-on-tone print for sails
    - 1⅛ yards teal print for boats, fish and quilt borders
    - ¼ yard light green print for fish appliqués
- ½ yard paper-backed fusible web
- 1⅞ yards 22-inch-wide firm fusible interfacing for the diaper stacker and wall organizer
- Tear-away embroidery stabilizer
- 1½ yards fleece for quilt and diaper stacker
- 2⅜ yards high-loft batting for bumper pad
- 2 yards ⅝-inch-wide hook-and-loop tape
- 3¾ yards ¼-inch-diameter piping cord
- 4¾ yards ¾-inch-diameter piping cord for bumper pad (may vary from pattern requirements)
- 2 (10 x 13½-inch) pieces of plastic needlepoint canvas
- #1 nickel safety pins for pin-basting the quilt layers
- Basic sewing supplies and equipment

Cutting
- Using rotary-cutting tools and, referring to the Nautical & Nice Cutting Chart on page 40, cut the pieces for the Fish and Sailboat blocks, and the quilt borders and binding.
- Set remaining fabrics aside and cut pieces as directed in the assembly directions for each item.

Patchwork Block Assembly
1. Using a sharp pencil, draw a diagonal line on the wrong side of each 4-inch yellow square and each 2-inch blue tone-on-tone square. With right sides together, sew each 4-inch yellow square to a 4-inch blue tone-on-tone square to make half-square triangle units. Stitch along the line as shown in Figure 1. Repeat with the 2-inch blue tone-on-tone squares and the teal print squares. Press as directed by the arrows on Figure 2. To eliminate bulk in the finished blocks, trim one layer of the fabric, leaving the other layer to help stabilize the block and keep it square.

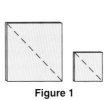

Figure 1

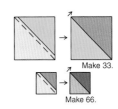

Make 33.

Make 66.

Figure 2

2. Referring to Figure 3, arrange the half-square triangle units with the remaining blue squares and rectangles, and the teal rectangles in the rows shown to make 33 sailboat blocks. Using ¼-inch-wide seams, sew the pieces together in rows, pressing the seams in the direction of the arrows. Sew the rows together and press. Choose three blocks for the diaper stacker and set the remaining blocks aside for the other projects.

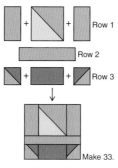

Figure 3

3. Sew a 1½ x 7-inch blue strip to the lower edge of one of the three blocks. Sew each of the remaining strips to the upper edge of a block. Set these blocks aside for the diaper stacker.

Quilt Assembly

Note: *Use ¼-inch-wide seam allowances.*

1. Trace 18 each of the fish head, body and tail onto the paper side of paper-backed fusible web. Leave a bit of margin between each piece in each fish. Cut apart in two groups of nine fish each.

2. Apply one set of tracings to the wrong side of the light green print and the remaining set to the wrong side of the teal print. Cut out the shapes and remove the backing paper.

3. Alternating colours and referring to the photo, arrange three fish on each 10 x 10½-inch blue print rectangle. Positioning of the fish can vary from block to block. Place the tip of a warm iron in the centre of each appliqué piece to fuse-baste them in place. Cover the fuse-basted fish appliqués with a damp press cloth and fuse in place following the manufacturer's directions.

4. Attach a rectangle of tear-away embroidery stabilizer to the wrong side of each block. Adjust the machine for a medium-width, closely spaced satin stitch and attach the appliqué presser foot if available. Satin-stitch over all raw edges on each fish. Remove the stabilizer.

5. Referring to the quilt photo for the direction of the stripes, cut (12) 2½ x 6½-inch strips and (12) 2 x 10½-inch strips from the striped fabric.

6. Sew the striped strips to six sailboat blocks as shown in Figure 4 (page 42) and press as directed by the arrows. Add the 2 x 10½-inch striped strips

Nautical & Nice Cutting Chart

Cut all strips across the fabric width. Strips will be approximately 40 to 42 inches long, depending on fabric width after preshrinking.

Fabric	No. of Strips	Strip Width	Crosscuts	
			No. to Cut	**Size**
Blue print	2	10½ inches	6 rectangles	10 x 10½ inches
	5	2½ inches	None	
Blue tone-on-tone print	4	4 inches	33 squares	4 x 4 inches
	10	2 inches	66 squares	2 x 2 inches
			66 rectangles	2 x 4 inches
	7	1½ inches	36 rectangles	1½ x 7 inches
Yellow	4	4 inches	33 squares	4 x 4 inches
Teal print	7	2 inches	66 squares	2 x 2 inches
			33 squares	2 x 4 inches
	5	3½ inches	See Quilt Assembly	

to the opposite edges of the block and press. The finished blocks should measure 10 x 10½ inches.

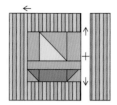

Figure 4

7. Arrange the sailboat and fish blocks in alternating fashion in four rows of three blocks each as shown in the photo. Sew the blocks together in rows and press the seams in opposite directions from row to row (Figure 5). Sew the rows together to complete the quilt top centre.

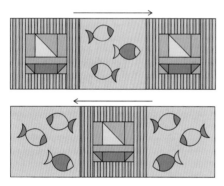

Figure 5

8. Sew three of the 3½-inch-wide teal border strips together using diagonal seams. Press the seams open. Measure the quilt top length through the centre and cut two strips this length from the long border strip. Sew the strips to the long edges of the quilt top, easing or stretching as needed. This method ensures a truly "square" quilt. Press the seams toward the borders.

9. Measure the quilt top width from border edge to border edge through the centre and use this measurement to cut two borders from the remaining 3½-inch-wide teal strips. Sew to the top and bottom edges of the quilt top and press the seams toward the borders.

10. Layer the quilt top with batting and backing, and pin-baste the layers together. Stitch in the ditch of all vertical and horizontal seams between the blocks and in the seams between the blocks

and borders. Do additional quilting in the blocks as desired. For example, stitch in the ditch of all seams in the pieced blocks and outline-stitch the appliquéd fish. Quilt the borders with a fish using the fish appliqué shape as a guide.

11. Machine-stitch ⅛ inch from the outer edges of the quilt through all layers. Trim the batting and backing even with the quilt-top edges.

12. Using bias seams, sew the 2½-inch-wide blue print strips together for the binding. Press the seams open. Fold the strip in half lengthwise with wrong sides together and press. Refer to binding instructions in General Instructions on page 9.

Bumper Pad Assembly

Note: *Use ¼-inch-wide seam allowances.*

1. Use the pattern pieces to cut bumper-pad tabs from the striped fabric. Also cut eight 2⅛ x 40½-inch strips.

2. Sew the remaining sailboat blocks together in four groups of six blocks each; press the seams in one direction. Compare each strip to the length of the bumper pad pattern piece, and if they are not as long as the pattern, add a strip of blue tone-on-tone print to one end of the strip to make it the appropriate length (40½ inches). Sew the four strips together and press the seams in one direction.

3. Sew the 2⅛ x 40½-inch striped strips together in sets of four to make two long strips. Press the seams in one direction. Sew the strips to the upper and lower edges of the patchwork strip; press the seams toward the strips.

4. Complete the bumper pad following the directions in the pattern guide sheet.

3. Position the patchwork faceup on the fleece and pin-baste the layers together.

4. Use the pattern pieces to cut the body of the diaper stacker and the bias for the corded piping from the remaining striped fabric. Cut interfacing as directed in the pattern.

5. Complete the diaper stacker following the pattern directions.

Wall Organizer Assembly

1. Cut and construct the wall organizer using the remaining blue print fabric and following the pattern directions.

2. Appliqué three fish along top of organizer following the appliqué directions for the quilt blocks. **Note:** *Since the front of the organizer is backed with a firm fusible interfacing, it is not necessary to back the appliqués with a tear-away stabilizer.* ✦

Diaper Stacker Assembly

1. Arrange the blocks and pieces for the upper front panel of the diaper stacker as shown in Figure 6; sew together using ¼-inch-wide seam allowances. Press.

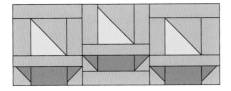

Figure 6

2. Position upper front panel pattern piece on the patchwork strip. If the strip is not wide enough to accommodate the pattern piece (due to cutting and piecing inaccuracies), cut a 2 x 18-inch strip from the blue tone-on-tone print and sew to the bottom edge of the strip. Reposition the pattern piece on the patchwork strip with the middle sailboat centred in the strip. Pin in place and cut out. Use the same pattern piece to cut the back upper panel from the blue print and a matching layer of fleece.

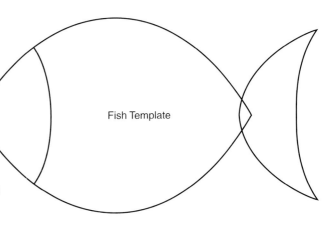

Fish Template

Dapper Diaper Bags

Mom can never have a diaper bag too large for the endless supplies necessary for travelling with baby. She'll thank you for making this oversized carryall!

DESIGN BY BETH WHEELER

Skill Level
Intermediate

Finished Size
Diaper Bag: 17 x 15 x 6 inches

Materials
- 1 yard light-value fabric for background panels
- ⅓ yard darker-value fabric for lower front and back and gusset
- 1 yard coordinating print for lining and outer back pocket
- Scraps for hair, pacifier and hair bow
- 18-inch square skin-tone fabric
- 2¾ yards (1-inch-wide) woven webbing for handles
- 3 packages coordinating piping
- ⅔ yard fusible fleece
- Scraps of fusible transfer web
- 1-inch plastic ring for pacifier
- 1 (¾-inch) shank button
- Rayon machine-embroidery thread to match appliqué fabrics
- Black and red permanent fabric markers
- Basic sewing supplies and equipment

Instructions
1. For lower front and back cut two darker-value fabric rectangles 5 x 18 inches. Cut two background panels from light-value fabric 12 x 18 inches. Cut bottom gusset from darker-value print 7 x 18 inches and two side gussets 7 x 16 inches. From lining fabric cut two outer back pocket pieces 10 x 11 inches and two inner pocket pieces 14 inches square. Cut two pieces for front and back lining 16 x 18 inches, two gusset pieces 7 x 16 inches and one 7 x 18 inches.

2. Cut handle webbing in two equal pieces. Position ends of one piece on right side of one background panel as shown in Figure 1. Stitch across lower ends ½ inch from bottom.

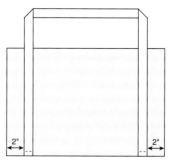

Figure 1

3. Stitch piping along one long edge of front lower piece. Stitch front panel and lower piece together.

4. Cut two fusible fleece 15 x 17 inches. Fleece is cut smaller than corresponding fabric to reduce bulk in seams. Centre and fuse one piece to wrong side of front. Topstitch close to edges of

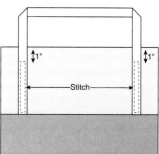

Figure 2

handle webbing, stopping 1 inch from top edge of background piece as shown in Figure 2 (page 44).

5. Trace appliqué shapes onto paper side of fusible transfer web; cut out, leaving roughly ½ inch margin around shapes.

6. Referring to photo, fuse to wrong side of selected fabrics according to manufacturer's directions; cut out on tracing line.

7. Position appliqué pieces and fuse in place. Satin-stitch around each appliqué piece with matching thread.

8. Stitch piping along one long edge of one outer back pocket piece. Place pocket pieces together with right sides facing. Stitch along one side of pocket, across top with piping and down the other side. Trim corners, turn right side out; press.

9. Stitch handles on remaining background panel as in Step 2. Stitch piping as in Step 3. Position

pocket on background panel between handles and with raw edges even. Baste through all layers close to raw edges. Stitch top panel and bottom piece together, right sides facing.

10. Centre and fuse remaining piece of fleece to wrong side of back unit. Topstitch close to both sides of handles as in Step 4. Topstitch close to edges of pocket, leaving top open. Topstitch down centre of pocket to divide in two sections.

11. Stitch piping around sides and bottom of front and back sections.

12. Stitch gusset pieces as shown in Figure 3. Press seams open. Cut fusible fleece 6 x 47 inches (to piece length, butt ends together). Centre and fuse to wrong side of gusset.

7" x 16"	7" x 18"	7" x 16"

Figure 3

13. Stitch front and back sections together with gusset between. Stitch piping around top edge.

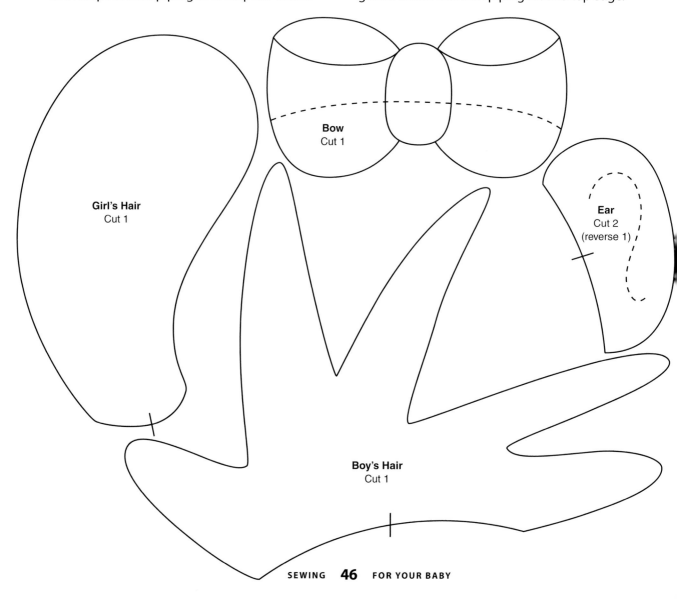

Bow
Cut 1

Girl's Hair
Cut 1

Ear
Cut 2
(reverse 1)

Boy's Hair
Cut 1

Lining

1. Stitch lining gusset together as shown in Figure 3.

2. Stitch inner pocket pieces together along three sides. Trim corners, turn right side out; press. Position even with bottom edge of one lining piece. Topstitch close to sides and bottom of pocket.

3. Stitch lining front and back sections together with gusset between.

4. Place bag inside lining, right sides together. Stitch around top, leaving an opening for turning. Trim corners; turn right side out through opening. Close opening.

Finishing

1. Fold back at each bottom and side seam, and topstitch through all layers close to edge. This helps the bag hold its shape and stand, empty or full. Topstitch around top of bag through handles and all layers as shown in Figure 4. Stitch an X in a box at the top of each handle to reinforce.

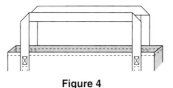

Figure 4

2. Add eyes, eyebrows and smile with black permanent fabric marker. Rub red permanent fabric marker on your index finger and immediately rub in a circular motion on cheek areas. Repeat for desired intensity.

Note: *Features may be embroidered if desired.*

3. Stitch plastic ring and button in place for pacifier. ✦

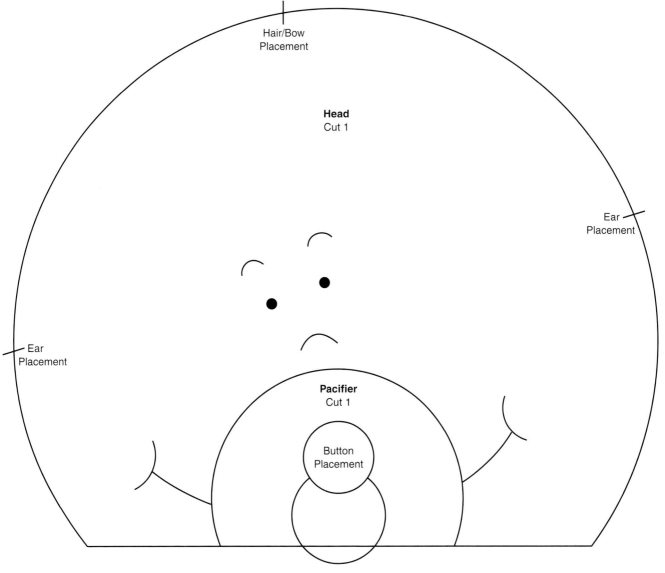

Hair/Bow
Placement

Head
Cut 1

Ear
Placement

Ear
Placement

Pacifier
Cut 1

Button
Placement

Spring Baby Bibs

Spring designs are easy to appliqué on these adorable bibs, perfect for baby's first outing.

DESIGNS BY CHERYL FALL

Skill Level
Beginner

Finished Size
One size fits most

Materials for Each
- Two 8½ x 10-inch pieces of white fabric
- One 8½ x 9-inch piece of fusible fleece
- Scraps of fabrics for appliqués
- One 5 x 9-inch piece of paper-backed fusible web
- 1 package Coats medium rickrack in desired colour
- 1 package desired-colour Coats extra-wide double-fold bias tape
- Coats Dual Duty Plus® all-purpose thread to match bias tape
- Clear Coats nylon monofilament
- Coats Colour Twist rayon thread in colours to match appliqué fabrics
- Basic sewing supplies and equipment

Candy Appliqué
Enlarge 200%

Bunny Appliqué
Enlarge 200%

Neck Edge Shaping

Corner Shaping

Instructions

1. Enlarge appliqué patterns 200 per cent. Trace appliqué patterns onto paper side of fusible web and cut out roughly. Fuse shapes to wrong sides of appliqué fabrics and cut out.

2. Fuse fleece to wrong side of one of the white pieces of fabric. Using corner and neck edge shaping patterns, round off all corners and cut out neck opening. This will be the bib front.

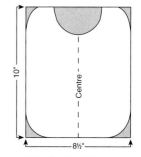

10"

Centre

8½"

Bib Cutting Diagram

3. For the candy bib, mark a line horizontally 1½ inches from bottom of bib front and mark a second line 3 inches from first line. Fuse candy appliqués centred between these lines.

4. For the bunny bib, mark a horizontal line 1½ inches from bottom of bib front. Fuse bunny above this line.

5. Machine appliqué all pieces in place using matching rayon threads and a medium-width satin stitch.

6. Using nylon monofilament and a narrow zigzag stitch, stitch rickrack along marked lines.

7. Place bib front and remaining piece of white fabric together, wrong sides facing. Pin layers together and stitch ⅛ inch from outside edge using all-purpose thread. Add a line of narrow zigzag stitches ¼ inch outside each piece of

rickrack. Trim backing fabric to the shape of bib front.

8. Using all-purpose thread and bias tape, bind outer edges of bib, leaving neck opening unbound.

9. Cut a 35-inch length of bias tape and fold in half to locate centre. Pin centre of bias tape to centre of neck edge, leaving ends extending from each end of neckline edge. Bind neck edge first, then stitch along doubled edges of tape to complete ties. Knot ends of ties. ◆

Quacker Cutie Bath Wrap

Baby will be adorable wrapped in this hooded towel after bath time. Make this bath wrap for your own sweet babe or for a shower gift. For gift giving, fold the towel and tie a big bow under the duck's chin.

DESIGN BY CAROL ZENTGRAF

Skill Level
Beginner

Finished Size
32 x 32 inches, excluding the hood

Materials
- 1 yard 44/45-inch-wide yellow terry cloth
- 2 (4 x 5¼-inch) rectangles orange microfibre fleece or washable felt for the duck's bill
- 2 (¾ x 1¼-inch) rectangles blue microfibre fleece for the eyes
- 1½ yards yellow double-fold bias binding
- Hook-and-loop-tape closure
- Basic sewing supplies and equipment

Cutting
From terry cloth:
- Cut one 34-inch square for the towel. Curve the corners as shown in Figure 1.

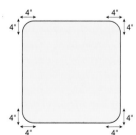

Figure 1

- Enlarge the hood pattern (Figure 2). Use the pattern to cut two hood pieces from the terry cloth.

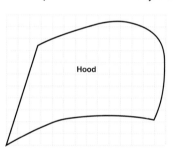

Hood

Figure 2
1 square = 1 inch

From orange fleece rectangles:
- Round the lower corners as shown in Figure 3 to make the duck's bill.

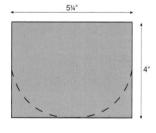

5¼"

4"

Figure 3

From blue fleece rectangles:
- Trim fabric into ovals for the eyes.

Assembly

Note: *Use ½-inch-wide seam allowances unless otherwise stated.*

1. Turn under and press a double ½-inch-wide hem on towel edges. Topstitch ⅜ inch from the turned edge through all layers.

2. Draw a circle with a 4-inch diameter in the centre of the towel. Fold the towel in half with the nap of the terry cloth running from the upper edge to the lower edge; cut the front opening along the fold. Open the square and cut out the circle to create the neck opening (Figure 4).

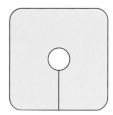

Figure 4

3. With right sides facing, sew the hood pieces together along the centre seam. Trim the seam allowance to ¼ inch, and then zigzag- or serge-finish the edges (Figure 5). Turn the hood right side out and press as needed.

Figure 5

4. With right sides together and front edges even, pin the hood to the neck edge; ease the hood as needed to fit. Stitch, trim and finish as described for the hood seam in step 3.

5. Pin the double-fold bias tape around the centre front and hood edges with the tape extending 1 inch past each lower edge. Zigzag along the folded edge through all layers to attach the tape. Turn under and press ½ inch at the end of each bias-tape extension. Turn again and sew in place on the inside at the lower front edges.

Note: *Refer to Figure 6 for steps 6 and 7.*

6. With right sides facing and using a ¼-inch-wide seam, sew or serge the orange fleece rectangles together along the curved edges. Turn right side out and finger-press the seam; topstitch a scant ¼ inch from the finished outer edge. Serge or machine-baste the short raw edges of the duck's bill together.

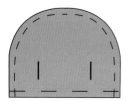

Figure 6

7. Mark ¾-inch-long nostril stitching lines, positioning them 1¼ inches from the side edges of the bill and ending ¾ inch from the straight edge of the bill. Machine-stitch the lines back and forth several times for emphasis (Figure 6).

8. Centre the duck's bill at the seam on the right side of the hood with the raw edges even with the finished edge. Stitch ¼ inch from the edges (Figure 7).

Figure 7   Figure 8

9. Turn the duck's bill over the seam edges and topstitch through all layers a scant ¼ inch from the seam line as shown in Figure 8.

10. Position the eyes ½ inch above the duck's bill and ¾ inch apart. Edgestitch in place, stitching twice for added security.

11. Sew a hook-and-loop tape closure to the towel at the neckline just below the hood seam line.

12. To fold the towel for gift giving, fold each side edge under twice until even with the head. Fold the lower edge up behind the head and wrap the ribbon around the folded towel; tie in a bow under the bill. ✦

Roly-Poly Lamb

This cuddly little lamb is constructed entirely of circles and sewn by hand.

DESIGN BY DIANA STUNELL-DUNSMORE

Skill Level
Beginner

Finished Size
Lamb: Approximately 17-inch circumference

Materials
- ⅓ yard white fleece
- ¼ yard black T-shirt knit
- 1 (⅝-inch) bell
- Scrap of ⅛-inch-wide pink ribbon
- 2 (3mm or 4mm) white beads or 6-strand white embroidery floss
- 3 strands of light pink embroidery floss
- Black and white all-purpose sewing thread
- Polyester fibrefill
- Sturdy sewing needle
- Needle-nose pliers
- Basic sewing supplies and equipment

Instructions
1. Trace and cut pieces as directed on patterns.
2. Using doubled white thread, run a gathering stitch close to the edge around the circumference of the lamb body. Place a very large handful of polyester fibrefill in the centre of the body circle and pull up the thread as tightly as possible; securely knot. The circle will not be closed because of the thickness of the fabric. Add more fibrefill if necessary to fill out body shape.
3. Using doubled black thread, run a gathering stitch close to the edge around the circumference of the lamb head. Place a small amount of polyester fibrefill in the centre of the head circle and pull up the thread as tightly as possible; securely knot. Take two long vertical stitches on the back of the head, and pull top and bottom of head together to give head a more oval shape.
4. Using doubled black thread, run a gathering stitch close to the edge around the circumference of each ear. Pull up the thread as tightly as possible; securely knot. The ears are not stuffed. Attach ears to back of head with hand stitches.
5. Referring to Figure 1, with white thread sew white beads to front of head for eyes. Insert needle from back of head and return to back of head to knot.
Note: To baby-proof, use white embroidery floss and make French knots with two wraps around the needle.

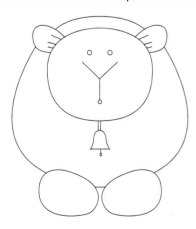

Figure 1

6. With 3 strands of light pink embroidery floss, embroider nose and mouth. Referring to Figure 2, bring needle up at A, down at B, leaving floss loose enough to form nose. Come up at C and bring floss over the A-B strands, pulling tightly enough to form a V. Go down at D. Come up again very near D and form a triple-wrapped French knot.

Figure 2

7. Thread the scrap of pink ribbon through bell loop. Fold ribbon in half and tack ends together on back of face.

8. With doubled white thread, position and sew head securely to body over fleece opening. Use needle-nose pliers to help pull the needle through the thick layers. Sew all around head two or three times. Leave bell and ears free.

9. Using doubled black thread, run a gathering stitch close to the edge around the circumference of one lamb foot. Place a very small amount of

polyester fibrefill in the centre of the foot circle and pull up the thread as tightly as possible; securely knot. Repeat for four feet.

10. Pin feet to bottom of body. Position with all four feet touching each other. With doubled black thread, sew each foot to body as shown in Figure 3.

11. Using doubled white thread, run a gathering stitch close to the edge around the circumference of lamb tail. Place a tiny amount of polyester fibrefill in the centre of the tail circle and pull up the thread as tightly as possible; securely knot, but do not cut thread. Sew tail securely to lamb's backside. ◆

Figure 3

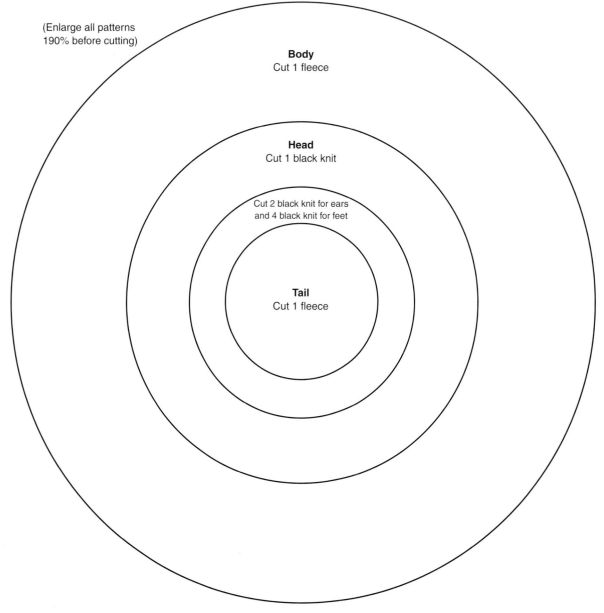

(Enlarge all patterns 190% before cutting)

Body
Cut 1 fleece

Head
Cut 1 black knit

Cut 2 black knit for ears
and 4 black knit for feet

Tail
Cut 1 fleece

Puppy Love

This cute little rug with its perky puppy head is sure to become Baby's first love. It's the perfect place for playtime stretching and snuggling.

DESIGN BY CAROL ZENTGRAF

Skill Level
Beginner

Finished Size
30 x 40 inches

Materials
- 2⅓ yards 60-inch-wide plush fleece fabric
- Scrap black fleece, washable felt or faux suede for nose
- 2 x 3-inch piece red fleece, washable felt or faux suede for tongue
- 1 set ⅞-inch-diameter animal eyes with safety shank
- Polyester fibrefill

Fake Fur

Try using fake fur instead of plush fleece fabric.

For cutting, simply trace around the pattern on the back side of the fake fur. Using a sharp pair of scissors, cut the knit backing of the fabric being careful not to clip the fur.

Loosen your tension and set a slightly longer stitch length. Sew fabric with right sides together.

Turn right side out, and using a small crochet hook or soft bristle brush, gently pull fur from the seam allowance. Lightly brush seam with your fingertips.

- Small dog collar (optional)
- Long dollmaker's or upholstery needle
- Basic sewing supplies and equipment

Cutting
Enlarge the patterns for head, body and ears on pattern tracing cloth or paper; cut out.

From the plush fleece:
- Cut one body top on fold.
- Cut two body bottoms, reversing one.
- Cut two heads, reversing one.
- Cut four ears, reversing two.

From scraps of fleece:
- Use the patterns to cut one tongue and one nose.

Assembly
Note: Use ½-inch-wide seam allowances.
1. Sew each set of ear pieces together, leaving the straight edge open. Turn right side out. Baste each ear to a head piece along centre line of dart. With right sides together, pin and sew the dart in the head, enclosing raw edges of the ear.
2. With right sides together and raw edges even all around, pin and sew the two head pieces together. Turn right side out. Turn under ¼ inch around the neck opening and hand-baste in place.
3. Make a tuck in the straight edge of the tongue and machine-stitch ⅛ inch from the raw edge. Centre the tucked edge of the tongue at the centre

of the muzzle across the muzzle seam. Securely hand-tack or machine-stitch the straight edge of the tongue in place.

4. Attach eyes at eye locations on each side of the head. Stuff the head with fibrefill and hand-sew the nose in place around the outer edges. Sew a second time for added security.

5. With right sides together, sew the body top and bottom together around outer edges. Turn right side out and slipstitch bottom seam closed. Stitch 3-inch-long lines from finished edge into paw to sculpt paws.

6. Centre and position the front edge of the puppy's neck 1½ inches from the front edge of the rug and pin in place all around. Using doubled thread, hand-stitch the neck edge to the body through both layers.

7. To sculpt the muzzle, thread the dollmaker's or upholstery needle with a long doubled strand of thread and knot the ends. Stitch into muzzle just above and to the left of the tongue. Bring the needle out above the left side of the nose

and pull the thread to sculpt. Stitch back in and across to bring the needle out at the opposite side of the nose. Pull on the thread and stitch. End by stitching out at the opposite side of the mouth. Pull tightly and secure thread. Repeat as necessary to achieve desired pucker.

8. Place dog collar around neck if desired.

Note: *The collar should be removed before use to prevent baby from becoming tangled in it or choking on it.* ◆

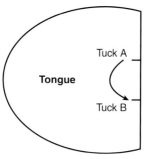

Puppy Love Patterns
Actual Size

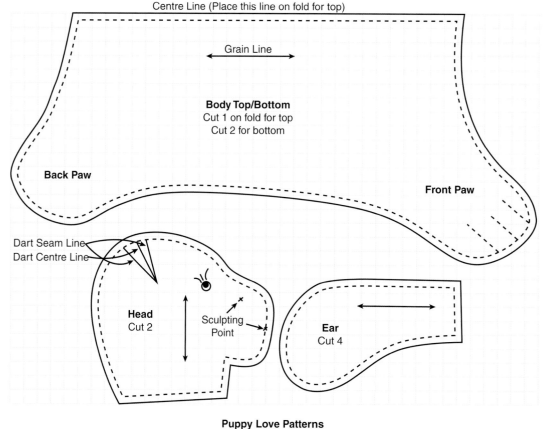

Puppy Love Patterns
1 square = 1 inch

Funny Bunny Wrist Rattle

This so-soft fleece bunny with a music button inside will keep Baby entertained for hours. Substitute a noisemaker for the music button if desired.

DESIGN BY JANIS BULLIS

Skill Level
Beginner

Finished Size
6 inches tall, including ears

Materials
- 2 (5 x 7-inch) rectangles soft polyester microfleece
- 1 (4 x 6-inch) rectangle polyester satin
- 2 (2 x 10-inch) strips cotton print for wristband
- 2 (1-inch) squares fusible interfacing
- ⅛ yard ¾-inch-wide elastic
- 2 safety eyes with locking backs, 12mm in diameter
- 1 noise rattler or music box
- Handful of fibrefill stuffing
- Bright pink embroidery floss (optional)
- Basic sewing supplies and equipment

Cutting
From fleece:
- Use patterns provided to cut two heads and two ears.

From satin:
- Use patterns provided to cut two ears.

Assembly
Note: *Use ¼-inch-wide seam allowances.*
1. With right sides together, sew each fleece ear to a satin ear along the curved edges; leave the bottom edge open for turning. Turn right side out and finger-press the finished edges.
2. Apply a 1-inch square of fusible interfacing to the eye area on the wrong side of each head piece. Make a small hole through the fleece and interfacing with a sharp scissors at the eye location on each head piece. Insert an eye through the hole and attach the locking device on the inside following the package directions.
Caution: *Do not substitute sew-on eyes because they are a choking danger if baby should pull them off.*
3. Fold each ear in half lengthwise with satin sides facing; machine-baste the raw edges together.
4. Stack and pin both ears to the upper edge of one head piece; baste in place (Figure 1). Pin the two heads together with raw edges even.

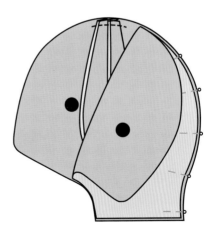

Figure 1

5. Sew the heads together, leaving the straight edge open for turning. Turn under ¼ inch around the opening raw edge and hand-baste in place (Figure 2).

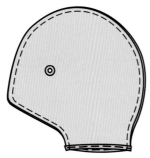

Figure 2

6. Turn the head right side out. Insert the music box or rattler and stuff the head to the desired firmness with polyester fibrefill.

7. With right sides facing, pin and stitch the two 2 x 10-inch cotton print strips together at both long edges. Turn right side out and press. Topstitch ¼ inch from each long edge.

8. Insert the elastic through one end and pin the elastic in place at the raw edges of the tube. Stitch. Thread the elastic through the strip and out the other end; stitch the elastic to the tube ends. Stitch the elasticized tube ends together with a ¼-inch-wide seam and press the seam open. Zigzag over the seam line, catching the seam allowances in the stitching (Figure 3).

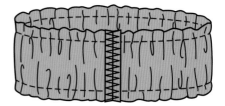

Figure 3

9. Position the bunny head on the wristband and slipstitch securely in place. Stitch a second time all around for added security. ***Optional:*** *Use bright pink embroidery floss to satin-stitch a pink nose on the bunny head.* ◆

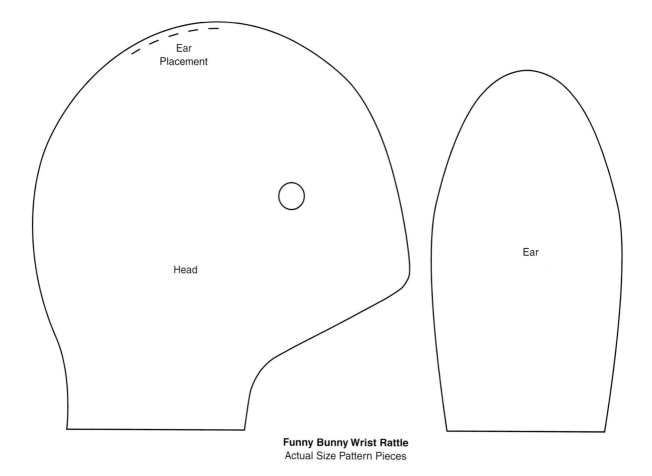

Ear Placement

Head

Ear

Funny Bunny Wrist Rattle
Actual Size Pattern Pieces

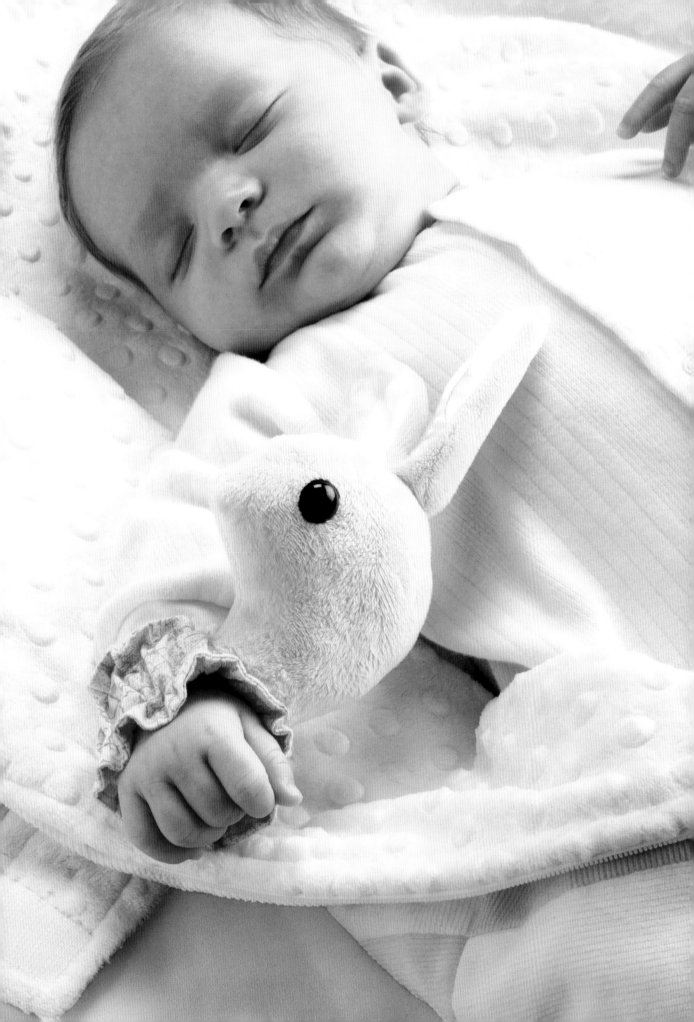

Play With My Heart

Brightly coloured appliqués and a soft, squeezable texture combine in this easy-to-make baby toy.

DESIGN BY REBECCA KEMP BRENT

Skill Level
Beginner

Finished Size
6 x 6 x 6 inches

Materials
- 45-inch-wide fabric:
    ¼ yard ⅛-inch red-check gingham
    ¼ yard red-and-white stripe
- Scrap fabric for appliqués:
    red solid and print for letters, cherries and heart
    green solid for leaf appliqués
- Fusible web
- Lightweight fusible batting
- Tear-away stabilizer
- 6 inches coordinating ⅝-inch-wide grosgrain ribbon
- Red all-purpose thread
- Green and red polyester machine appliqué and embroidery thread
- Embroidery bobbin thread
- Polyester fibrefill
- Basic sewing supplies and equipment

Cutting
From red-check gingham:
- Cut four 6½ x 6½-inch squares.

From red-and-white stripe:
- Cut two 6½ x 6½-inch squares.

From fusible batting:
- Cut six 6½ x 6½-inch squares.

From scrap fabric for appliqués:
- Cut three 2⅝-inch circles for cherries.
- Apply fusible web to scraps. Use patterns provided to cut letters, hearts and leaves.

Assembly
Note: *Use ¼-inch-wide seam allowances.*

1. For cherry yo-yo appliqués, press under raw edges ¼ inch. Using a double strand of thread, hand-sew a running stitch ¹⁄₁₆ inch from pressed edge, finishing on the wrong side. Pull thread tails to gather circle. Tie ends securely and trim close to knot. Flatten yo-yos slightly with gathers centred; finger-press.

2. Fuse interfacing to wrong sides of 6½-inch gingham and stripe squares.

3. Using cherry block pattern as a guide, lightly sketch cherry stems on right side of one prepared gingham square using a removable marking tool.

4. Slide a layer of tear-away stabilizer under fabric. Using green embroidery thread and a triple straight stitch (also called straight stretch or bean stitch), stitch cherry stems.

5. Fuse appliqué leaves on block at stem intersection. Stitch a vein in each leaf. Change machine stitch setting to satin zigzag 3mm wide and 0.3–0.4mm long. Sew around each leaf, anchoring stitches at beginning and end.

6. Pin cherry yo-yos over ends of stems. Using red embroidery thread, select an appliqué or blind-hem stitch. Stitch around yo-yos so stitches just catch

Figure 1

edges (Figure 1, page 62). Tear away stabilizer. Place block facedown on padded surface, cover with press cloth and press.

7. Fuse heart appliqué to a second gingham square. Place a layer of stabilizer under block. Select a scalloped satin stitch 6.0mm wide and 0.3–0.4mm long. Stitch around heart, covering raw edges with decorative stitch. Remove stabilizer and press as in step 6.

8. Fuse letter appliqués to remaining gingham blocks. Using stabilizer and red thread, stitch around edges with a zigzag stitch. Remove stabilizer and press. ***Note:*** *For the smoothest satin edge, stitch first with a 4mm wide, 0.3–0.4mm-long zigzag, and then stitch again with a slightly wider satin zigzag (4.5mm). Stitch slowly and turn the fabric often to sew around curves.*

9. Referring to Figure 2, sew appliquéd gingham blocks right sides together beginning and ending seams ¼ inch from raw edges. Sew stripe blocks to each side of cherry block. Fold ribbon in half to form a loop; pin to stripe block as shown with ends of ribbon even with raw edges of block.

10. Sew ends of gingham strip together; then sew top stripe block to top edges of gingham blocks, pivoting at each corner and catching ribbon ends in stitching. Sew bottom square, leaving an opening at the centre of one side for turning.

11. Turn right side out. Stuff with fibrefill. Hand-stitch opening closed. ✦

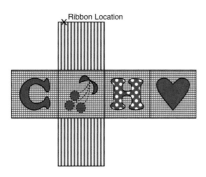

Figure 2

Letter Perfect

Personalize the block with initials or make a complete alphabet set! It's easy to convert most computer fonts to patterns for large appliquéd letters.

1. Open a new blank document and type the desired letter.

2. Drag the cursor over the letter to highlight it.

3. Click the drop-down menu arrow next to the font name on the toolbar. A list of available fonts will appear. Use the keyboard arrows to move down the list; then click on the desired font.

4. Click inside the box that displays the font size. Type in a large number and press Enter. Experiment with different font sizes. The same numerical size in different fonts creates different letter sizes.

5. With the new letter highlighted, right-click on the letter and choose "Font" from the pop-up menu to open the font formatting dialogue box. In the middle section, click on the box beside "Outline," and then click OK. The large letter should appear in white with a black outline.

6. Print the letter on paper, freezer paper, adhesive template sheets or fusible tear-away stabilizer to create the pattern.

Note: *Some fonts will not convert to the outline form. In that case, use the font formatting dialogue box to colour the letter a pale grey to use less ink in printing.*

Letter H

Letter C

Heart

Sewing Room Decor

Keep your sewing notions and protect your sewing machine with a coordinated cover.

DESIGNS BY CHERYL FALL

Skill Level
Beginner

Finished Sizes
Machine Cover: 18 x 13 x 8 inches
Organizer: 13 x 17 inches
Pincushion: 6 inches square

Materials
- 44/45-inch-wide cotton fabrics:
    - 2 yards of blue-on-white print
    - ½ yard of white-on-blue print
    - ½ yard of light blue-on-navy print
    - ¼ yard of medium blue print
- 2 yards of fusible fleece
- Paper-backed fusible web
- White all-purpose thread
- Clear nylon monofilament
- Bias corded piping:
    - 2 packages blue
    - 1 package white
- 1 package white extra-wide double-fold bias tape
- 1 skein matching blue 6-strand embroidery floss
- 6 white ¾-inch buttons
- 2 white ½-inch buttons
- Basic sewing supplies and equipment

Cutting
Note: *Use ¼ inch for seam allowances. Stitch pieces right sides together unless otherwise stated.*

For machine cover:
- From blue-on-white print fabric, cut four pieces each 18½ x 13½ inches, cut two pieces each 8½ x 44 inches for outer cover and lining.
- From fusible fleece, cut two pieces each 18½ x 13½ inches, cut one piece 8½ x 44 inches, cut one piece 6¼ x 18½ inches for pocket.
- From white-on-blue print fabric, cut two pieces each 12½ x 6½ inches for end pockets.
- From light blue-on-navy print fabric, cut one piece 12½ x 6½ inches for centre pocket.

For organizer:
- From blue-on-white print fabric, cut two pieces each 13½ x 17½ inches for sides.
- From fusible fleece, cut one piece 13½ x 17½ inches.
- From white-on-blue print fabric, cut one piece 8 x 13½ inches for pocket.
- From light blue-on-navy print fabric, cut one piece 8 x 13½ inches for pocket.
- From medium blue print fabric, cut one piece 8 x 13½ inches for pocket, cut two pieces each 3½ x 8 inches for hanging tabs.

For pincushion:
- From medium blue print fabric, cut one piece 6½ inches square for back.
- From white-on-blue print fabric, cut one piece 4½ inches square.
- From blue-on-white print fabric, cut three pieces each 1½ x 7 inches.

Assembly

Machine Cover Assembly

1. Fuse fleece to wrong sides of matching outer cover pieces.

2. Using a saucer or curved template as a pattern, round off top left and right corners on side pieces for outer cover and for lining.

3. Stitch matching long edges of pocket pieces together.

4. Fuse pocket fleece to lower half of assembled pocket. Fold assembled pocket in half, wrong sides together, forming an 18½ x 6¼-inch piece. Press.

5. Using white all-purpose thread, topstitch ¼ inch from seam lines of pockets to secure layers together. Pin pocket to right side on bottom half of one outer cover side. Using monofilament thread, stitch along each seam line on pocket.

6. Stitch piping around top and side edges of each outer cover side piece.

7. Stitch side and top edges of each outer cover side piece to long edges of 44-inch outer cover piece. Clip curved seam allowances. Repeat with lining pieces.

8. Stitch piping around bottom edge of assembled outer cover. Place outer cover and lining right sides together. Stitch around bottom edge, leaving a 4-inch opening for turning. Turn right side out and hand-stitch opening closed.

9. Stitch one ½-inch button to top of each pocket seam.

Organizer Assembly

1. Fuse matching fleece piece to wrong side of one side piece for front.

2. Fuse one fleece piece to wrong side of each pocket piece in same manner as machine cover pocket. Fold one pocket piece in half, right sides together and stitch long raw edges together. Turn right side out. Repeat on each pocket.

3. Using monofilament thread, stitch ⅛ inch from the bottom edge and ¼ inch from the top folded edge of each pocket.

4. Pin one pocket along bottom edge of organizer front and stitch in place along side and bottom edges of pocket.

5. Position remaining pockets on front, spacing them 1¼ inches apart (Figure 1). Stitch side and bottom edges of pockets in place.

6. For pocket dividers, evenly space two stitching lines on bottom and top pockets, and one stitching line across centre of middle pocket. Stitch one button at top of each stitching line on each pocket.

Figure 1

7. For hanging tabs, fold medium blue fabric pieces in half lengthwise and stitch long edges together. Turn right sides out. With seam at centre back, press. Fold tabs in half, forming loops, and baste ends to top edge of organizer back side, 4 inches apart.

8. Baste organizer sides, wrong sides together. Bind edges with double-fold bias.

Pincushion Assembly

1. For front, stitch 7-inch strips to two opposite edges on 4½-inch square (Figure 2). Trim ends of strips. Press seams toward centre.

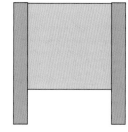 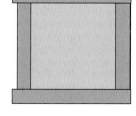

Figure 2   **Figure 3**

2. Stitch remaining 7-inch strips to other two edges of 4½-inch square and ends of strips (Figure 3). Press seams toward centre. Trim ends of strip.

3. Cut a piece from fleece to match assembled front. Fuse to wrong side of front. Stitch white piping around edge of front.

4. Stitch front and back together, leaving an opening on one edge for turning. Trim corners. Turn right side out. Stuff with fibrefill. Hand-stitch opening closed.

5. Stitch button to centre of front through all layers of pincushion. ◆

Sewing Room Accessories

Use the decorative stitches on your sewing machine to create these great accessories for your sewing space.

DESIGNS BY BROTHER INTERNATIONAL CORP.

Skill Level
Beginner

Finished Sizes
Caddy: 18 x 19 inches
Scissors Cover: fits up to 9-inch shears
Basket Cover: adjustable

Materials
- 1½ yards of burgundy 44/45-inch-wide cotton fabric
- 1 yard of burgundy quilted cotton fabric
- 1½ yards of fusible stabilizer
- Burgundy all-purpose sewing thread
- 2 yards ½-inch-wide gold ribbon
- Gold metallic heavy braid
- 1-inch plastic ring
- 3-inch gold tassel
- Fabric marking pencil
- Gold metallic machine embroidery thread
- Rayon decorative machine threads in light and dark shades of each pink and green

Instructions
Note: *Draw triangle pattern according to Figure 1. Cut out patterns for scissors pocket front and back. Use ¼ inch for seam allowances. Stitch pieces right sides together unless otherwise stated.*

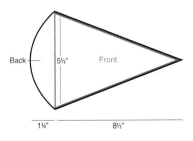

Back — 5½" — Front
1¾"   8½"

Figure 1

Cutting
- From each burgundy fabric and stabilizer, cut one piece each 20 x 28 inches (for caddy).
- From burgundy fabric, cut one 18-inch square (for basket cover)
- From quilted burgundy fabric, cut two pieces according to scissors pocket back.

For basket cover:
- Measure depth and width of basket and total these numbers. Add 4 inches to this total. Measure the depth and length of basket and total these numbers. Add 4 inches to this total.
- Using dimensions from last step, cut two pieces from non-quilted burgundy fabric.
- From stabilizer, cut one piece to match cover piece.

Caddy Assembly
1. Fuse stabilizer to wrong side of non-quilted fabric piece.

2. For decorative stitch guide lines, using fabric pencil, mark a line across piece 20 inches from one short end. Draw lines from corner to corner, forming an X in this marked area. Mark edges at 3-inch intervals and draw diagonal lines using marks.

3. Using built-in decorative stitches and metallic gold thread, stitch across each diagonal line, forming diamonds.

4. Using built-in alphabets and metallic gold thread, stitch sewing words at centre of desired diamonds. Decorate remaining diamonds with built-in embroidery designs and rayon threads. ***Note:*** *Rose design on photographed model is from Brother embroidery card No. 20.*

5. Stitch embroidered piece and quilted piece together, leaving an opening for turning. Clip corners. Turn. Press. Stitch opening closed.

6. Fold plain end of piece up 7 inches to form pocket. Pin in place. Topstitch around piece ¼ inch in from edge.

7. Stitch vertical lines along pocket to divide pocket for various size pockets.

Basket Cover Assembly

1. Fuse stabilizer to wrong side of one cover piece.

2. Decorate stabilized piece in same manner as caddy.

3. Serge pieces wrong sides together, or stitch pieces right sides together leaving an opening on one edge for turning; clip corners; turn; stitch opening closed. Edgestitch piece.

4. Place cover in basket. Pull one corner at a time and tie with 10-inch piece of ribbon.

Scissors Cover Assembly

1. Fuse stabilizer to wrong side of one pocket front piece. Decorate piece with built-in stitches in same manner as caddy.

2. Stitch pocket front pieces together. Trim seam allowance at point. Turn. Repeat with pocket back pieces.

3. Matching bottom point, place pocket front and back pieces together. Topstitch ¼ inch in from side edges.

4. Cover ring with metallic braid. Tack ring to top edge of cover. Tack tassel to bottom point of cover. ◆

Decorative Serger Cover

A serger is for more than just finishing seams. Have fun embellishing this unique serger cover.

DESIGN BY SARA BOUGHNER

Skill Level
Intermediate

Finished Size
Fits standard-size serger

Materials
- Base fabric:
    - 2 (14 x 13½-inch) rectangles for side panels
    - 37 x 16-inch piece for main cover body
- Lining fabric:
    - 2 (14 x 13½-inch) rectangles for side panels
    - 37 x 16-inch piece for main cover body
- Contrast fabric
- 2 yards 1½-inch-wide bias-cut strips for piping
- Serger
- Serger piping foot
- Decorative serger threads
- 2 yards narrow piping
- ½-inch-wide Steam-A-Seam2
- Fusible thread

Cutting
On each side panel piece, make the following cuts with right side up:
- Measure and mark 5¼ inches up from the bottom right corner.
- Measure and mark 9¾ inches in from top left corner.
- Using a ruler, draw a straight line from one mark to the other. Cut on the line, removing the top right corner.

Assembly
Note: *PFAFF creative coverlock [4874] was used for model project.*

1. Sew together bias-cut strips for piping using a mitred seam. Set aside.

2. Set serger for decorative stitch No. 28. This is a 10-thread decorative cover stitch. For this stitch, use the standard blue foot, lower the upper knife and attach the sewing table and decorative thread guides. The LCD display shows the required setup. Do a few rows of practice stitching to check threading, tension, balance and thread choice. Or follow your serger manufacturer's directions to do a cover stitch of your choice. Or simply use a decorative stitch on your sewing machine, if your serger does not do the cover stitch.

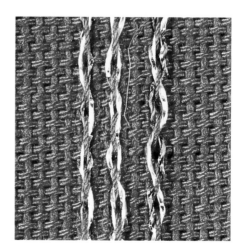

3. Change setting for another decorative stitch No. 28 or adjust your serger for Flat Lock by referring to your machine's instruction manual. On 37 x 16-inch

rectangle of main-cover body fabric, sew stitch No. 28 (Flat Lock) in vertical rows as shown, about every 3 inches. **Note:** *Stitch No. 22 was used for model project.* Sew horizontal rows, completing the grid pattern on the main portion of the serger cover.

4. Attach the piping foot and set the machine for a narrow overedge seam or refer to your serger's instruction manual and adjust your serger to an overedge finish. You may also use a zipper foot and straight stitch on your sewing machine to create piping.

5. Fold bias-cut strips over the narrow piping and place underneath the foot with the piping in the groove on the left side of the foot. Serge, encasing the piping in the fabric.

6. With right sides together, pin the side panels to the decorated main cover body piece, sandwiching the piping between the two. Stitch using the narrow overedge seam.

7. Remove the piping foot and put the standard foot back on. Using the same narrow overedge stitch, construct the lining by pinning and sewing the side panels of lining fabric to the main piece of lining fabric.

8. With right sides together, slip the cover exterior inside the cover lining and sew around the bottom edge to attach the two pieces, leaving an opening to turn. Turn right side out and press.

9. Fuse the opening closed using a piece of ½-inch-wide Steam-A-Seam2. Topstitch around the bottom edge using a 2-needle cover hem for a professional finish.

Embellish
1. Cut several randomly shaped appliqué pieces from the contrast fabric.

2. Prepare the serger for a wide overedge seam. Thread as follows:
- Serger thread in both needles
- Candlelight decorative thread in the upper looper
- Fusible thread in the lower looper

3. Test the stitch for proper threading and balance on a scrap of fabric before stitching project.

4. With right side up, serge around all edges of appliqué pieces. Trim thread tails away.

5. Position the appliqué pieces as desired and fuse in place. ◆

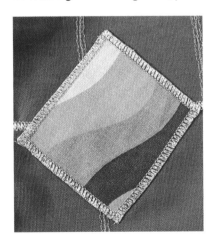

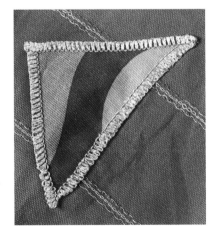

Chair Arm Sewing Caddy

Keep your sewing tools handy in this quick-to-make organizer. It's always ready to move when you are—from room to room, to the car or the doctor's office.

DESIGN BY KAREN MEAD

Skill Level
Beginner

Finished Size
Caddy: Approximately 8 x 20 inches

Materials
- ½ yard tan plaid flannel
- ¼ yard tea-dyed muslin
- 2-inch lace doily
- 5-inch lace doily
- Brown 6-strand embroidery floss
- 5 small buttons
- Polyester fibrefill
- All-purpose thread to match fabrics
- ¼ yard thin batting
- Water-soluble marker
- Basic sewing supplies and tools

Instructions
Note: *Use ¼-inch seam allowances throughout.*
1. Trace and cut fabrics as directed on patterns.
2. Trace compartment stitching lines and words onto front pocket muslin with water-soluble marker.
3. Referring to photo, stitch doilies in place.
4. With 2 strands of brown embroidery floss stitch words with running stitch. Add buttons.
5. Place two muslin pocket pieces wrong sides together and baste around outside edge. Cut strip of flannel 2 x 9 inches. Place facedown along top of pocket front. Stitch, then fold to back, turning raw edge under ¼ inch. Slipstitch in place. Machine-stitch along compartment lines.
6. Place completed pocket on front of flannel caddy piece. Baste in place.
7. Cut one muslin piece, using pattern, for pincushion. Using caddy pattern as a guide, determine placement for pincushion. Fold pincushion piece down toward pocket and stitch across. Fold pincushion back in place. Fold remaining long edge of pincushion under ¼ inch and stitch to caddy. Stuff with polyester fibrefill.
8. Place two flannel caddy pieces right sides together. Add batting piece on bottom. Stitch around sides and pocket, making a tuck at centres of pincushion when sewing over stuffed pocket. Leave top open. Clip seams, turn and slipstitch open end to finish. ◆

**Chair Arm Sewing Caddy
Pincushion**
Enlarge 150% before cutting for full-sized pattern. Cut 1 muslin

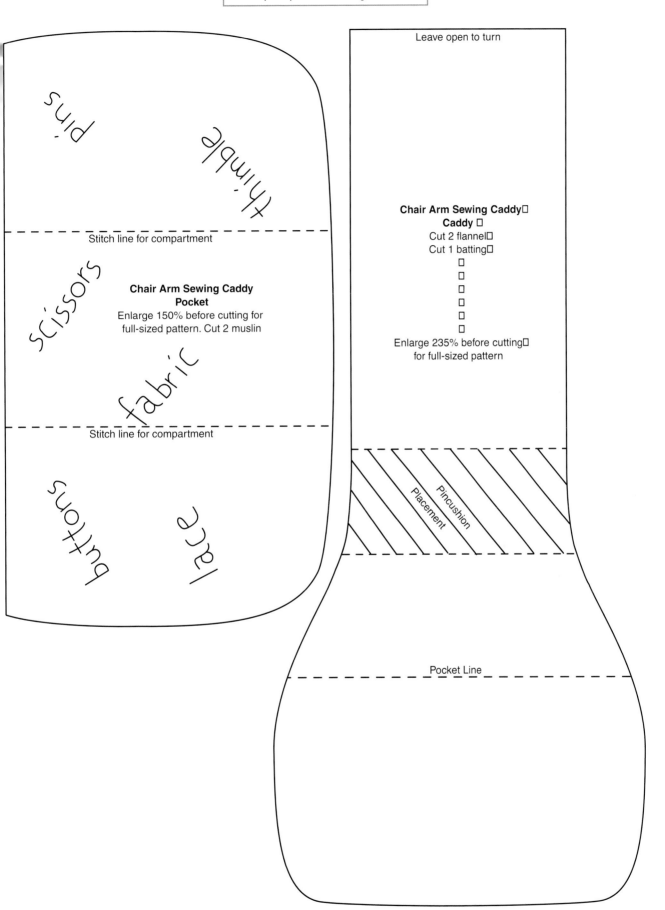

Leave open to turn

pins

thimble

Stitch line for compartment

scissors

**Chair Arm Sewing Caddy
Pocket**
Enlarge 150% before cutting for
full-sized pattern. Cut 2 muslin

fabric

Stitch line for compartment

buttons

lace

**Chair Arm Sewing Caddy
Caddy**
Cut 2 flannel
Cut 1 batting

Enlarge 235% before cutting
for full-sized pattern

Pincushion
Placement

Pocket Line

Pincushion Doll

A pincushion bustle at the back of her pretty floral-print apron makes this little lady quite useful as she fits right into place in the sewing room.

DESIGN BY VELETA "SAM" STAFNEY

Skill Level
Beginner

Finished Size
Doll: Approximately 16 inches

Materials
- 1 plastic 2-litre soda bottle
- ¼ yard white felt
- ⅔ yard pastel floral-on-white fabric
- ½ yard mauve-and-white stripe fabric
- ½ yard (½-inch-wide) white ruffled eyelet lace
- 1 (6-inch) burgundy heart-shaped Battenberg lace doily
- 2 yards (⅝-inch-wide) rose ribbon
- Brown tightly curled hair
- 1 (2-inch) wooden ball
- 1 (3½-inch-diameter) firm plastic-foam ball
- 6 inches gold 28-gauge wire
- Gold sewing scissors
- Polyester fibrefill
- 2 cups plastic pellets
- Skin-tone and rose acrylic paint
- Black fine-point permanent marker
- All-purpose thread to match fabrics
- Cotton swab
- Glue gun or tacky glue
- Serrated knife
- Air-drying disappearing marker
- Basic sewing supplies and tools

Instructions
Note: Use ¼-inch seam allowance unless otherwise noted.

1. Pour plastic pellets into bottle. Glue around inside of bottle cap and replace.

2. Cut two pieces 8¼ x 13 inches from white felt. Round off corners on one edge of each piece as shown in Figure 1. Pin felt together and sew both long side seams, leaving open at top and 3 inches along centre bottom. Turn right side out. Run a basting stitch along both openings. Pull 3-inch opening gathers tight and knot. Slip bottle inside. Pull remaining gathers tight around neck of bottle and knot threads.

Figure 1

3. Paint the wooden ball with skin-tone acrylic paint. When dry, draw eyes, eyelashes and nose with permanent marker, referring to photo for placement. Apply blush to cheeks with cotton swab and rose acrylic paint. When dry, glue head to top of bottle cap.

4. From mauve-and-white stripe fabric cut one piece 12½ x 42½ inches for petticoat. Sew short edges together. Turn right side out. For hem, fold under one raw edge ¼ inch; press. Turn under again, press and stitch. Run a basting stitch along other raw edge. Place dress over bottle and pull gathers tight under neck of bottle. Knot threads and spot with glue to secure.

5. From pastel floral fabric cut one 12¼ x 42½-inch piece for dress. Sew short ends together and turn

right side out. Fold under one raw edge ¼ inch; press. Turn under again, press and stitch. Run a basting stitch along raw edge, place dress over petticoat and pull gathers tight under head. Knot threads and spot with glue.

6. Cut a 5 x 15-inch piece of floral fabric for arms. Fold piece in half lengthwise and stitch. Turn right side out and run a basting stitch across arm centre. Pull gathers tight and knot. Lightly stuff each arm (either side of gathers). Overlap raw edges of both arms and run a basting stitch through all layers. Pull gathers tight and knot. Place arms over head and glue ends to back of dress.

7. Cut a slit in heart-shaped doily from point to centre. Cut a 1-inch circle at centre as shown in Figure 2. Place collar around neck with slit in back. Spot with glue to hold.

Figure 2

8. Wrap a strand of hair loosely around four fingers 10 times. Twist in centre and glue to top of head. Continue gluing hair to head, filling in sides and back. Clip any loose strands and spot with glue to hold.

9. Cut three 9-inch circles from pastel floral fabric. Right sides facing, sew two circles together around outer edge. Carefully cut a 2-inch slit in centre of one circle and turn right side out; press. Run a basting stitch around circle 1 inch from outer edge. Pull up gathers slightly, add some stuffing and fit to top of head. Add more stuffing and adjust gathers if needed. Knot threads and glue bonnet to top of head.

10. Run a basting thread along outer edge of remaining circle.

With serrated knife, cut foam ball in half and discard one half. Place ball, rounded side down, in centre of fabric circle. Pull up gathers and knot threads. Adjust gathers evenly around edge of ball. Glue eyelet lace around outer inside edge of ball. Glue flat side of ball to back of dress, right below waist.

11. Cut 12-inch piece of ⅝-inch-wide rose ribbon. Loop over centre of arm, through scissors and tie a bow. Angle-cut ribbon ends. Cut 1 yard of rose ribbon and make a six-loop bow. Wrap centre with wire and twist to secure. Cut off excess wire. Angle-cut ribbon ends. Glue to top of pincushion. Tie two small bows and angle-cut ends. Glue one to top of bonnet and one to front of doily at neck. ✦

Tea Time

Brighten your table and your day with a relaxing cup of tea. This simple pieced tea cozy and coordinating hot pads are serged quickly and easily. Take a break from your busy schedule and enjoy the relaxing effects of tea with a friend.

DESIGNS BY AGNES MERCIK

Skill Level
Intermediate

Finished Sizes
Cozy: 12 x 15 inches
Potpourri Pocket: 7½ inches square
Hot Pad: 5½ inches square

Materials
- 44/45-inch-wide cotton fabrics:
    ½ yard each of 4 coordinating prints
    ½ yard muslin
    ⅜ yard coordinating-colour faux suede (piping may be substituted for suede)
- Sewing thread to match fabrics
- ½ yard thermal fleece
- Potpourri
- Serger
- Basic sewing supplies and equipment

Cutting
For cozy:
- From colour A fabric, cut one piece 5 inches square.
- From colour B fabric, cut one piece 2 x 5 inches, cut one piece 2 x 6½ inches.
- From colour C fabric, cut one piece 2 x 8 inches, cut one piece 2 x 6½ inches.

- From colour D fabric, cut two pieces each 6½ x 8½ inches, cut two pieces each 4 x 11 inches, cut one piece 12¼ x 15¼ inches for cozy back.
- From thermal fleece, cut two pieces each 12¼ x 15¼ inches for cozy lining.
- For optional suede piping, cut ½-inch wide strips from suede fabric. Cut one strip ½ x 2 inches for top loop.

For potpourri pocket:
- From colour A fabric, cut one piece 5 inches square for centre, cut two pieces each 8 inches square for lining.
- From colour B fabric, cut one piece 2 x 5 inches, cut one piece 2 x 6½ inches.
- From colour C fabric, cut one piece 2 x 8 inches, cut one piece 2 x 6½ inches.
- From colour D fabric, cut four pieces each 1¼ x 8 inches.
- From thermal fleece, cut one piece 8 inches square for back.
- From muslin, cut two pieces each 8 inches square for potpourri pillow.

For hot pad:
- From colour A fabric, cut one piece 4 inches square.

- From colour B fabric, cut two pieces each 1¼ x 6 inches.
- From colour C fabric, cut two pieces each 1¼ x 8 inches.
- From colour D fabric, cut four pieces each 1 x 8 inches.
- From thermal fleece, cut one piece 8 inches square for back.

Cozy Assembly

1. Working in log cabin construction and adding suede strips as you work, serge strips around centre square as shown in assembly diagram.
2. Serge colour D pieces in place as shown.
3. Trim top corners of back and lining pieces as shown in diagram.
4. Trim assembled front to match back piece.
5. Serge a lining piece to wrong side of front and back. Adding suede strip and folded top loop to seam, serge front and back right sides together. Turn.

Hot Pad Assembly

1. Assemble pad front in same manner as cozy centre. Serge colour D strips in place trimming excess ends of strips away as you work.
2. Serge front and back right sides together, leaving an opening for turning. Turn. Hand-sew opening closed.

Potpourri Pocket Assembly

1. Assemble pocket front in same manner as cozy centre. Serge colour D strips in place trimming excess ends of strips away as you work.
2. Serge a lining piece to wrong side of front and back along one edge only. Turn right sides out. Press.
3. Serge raw edges of front and back right sides together. Turn.
4. Stitch message, if desired, on one pillow side piece. Serge pillow sides right sides together, leaving an opening for turning. Turn. Fill with potpourri. Hand-sew opening closed. ◆

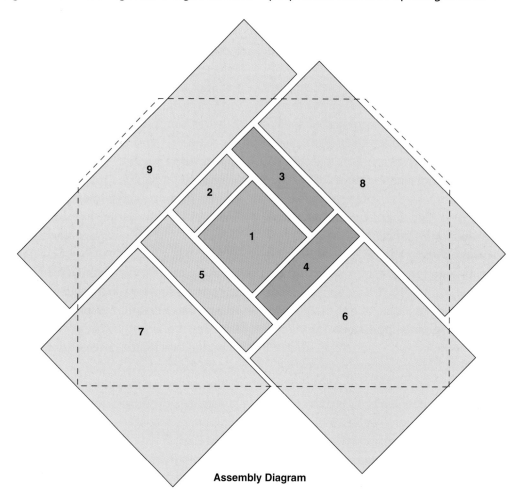

Assembly Diagram

Kitchen Caddy

This magnetic pocket organizer attaches to your refrigerator. No more excuses for losing things!

DESIGN BY JANE SCHENCK

Skill Level
Beginner

Finished Size
15½ x 19 inches

Materials
- ½ yard print 44/45-inch-wide decorator fabric
- ½ yard of contrasting print fabric
- 1 yard 22-inch-wide heavyweight nonwoven stabilizer
- 1½ yards of iron-on fusible web
- 56¼-inch piece of adhesive-backed magnetic strip
- Glue gun and glue sticks

Cutting
- From stabilizer and print fabric, cut two pieces each 18 x 20 inches.
- Use fusible web to attach print fabric to one side of each piece of stabilizer.
- From one piece of fabric-covered stabilizer, cut one piece 15½ x 19 inches for caddy backing.
- From remainder of fabric-covered stabilizer, cut one piece 6½ x 4 inches for coupon pocket, cut one piece 2¾ x 4 inches for scissors pocket, cut one piece 2 x 4 inches for bottle opener pocket, cut one piece 4½ x 6½ inches for pencil/ pen pocket, cut one piece 11 x 8½ inches for calendar pocket, cut one piece 4½ x 4½ inches for notepad pocket.

Assembly
1. Fuse contrasting fabric to uncovered side of caddy backing piece.
2. Machine-topstitch around outside edge of caddy backing piece and across top edge of each pocket.
3. Position pockets on background as shown in Figure 1 and topstitch in place. Stitch through centre of pencil/pen pocket.

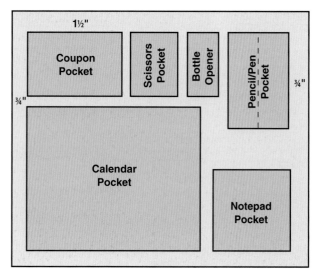

Figure 1

4. Cut magnetic strips into three pieces each 18¾ inches long. Peel off paper backing and place two strips across top and one across the bottom of caddy backing (for added hold, magnetic strips may be hot-glued onto back of caddy). ✦

Romance in the Kitchen

Add sugar and spice to your kitchen when you sew a matching heart-appliquéd three-piece set.

DESIGNS BY AGNES MERCIK

Skill Level
Beginner

Finished Sizes
Dish Towel: 17¾ x 28¼ inches, including lace trim
Oven Mitt: 6 x 12½ inches, without hanging loop
Pot Holder: 8¼ x 8¼ inches

Materials for One Each Dish Towel, Oven Mitt & Pot Holder
- 44/45-inch-wide 100 per cent cotton fabric:
    1¼ yards solid for dish towel
    ½ yard quilted for oven mitt and pot holder*
    ¼ yard each of at least 3 coordinating prints
      for bias binding, loops and appliqués
- ¼ yard quilted Teflon fabric*
- Paper-backed fusible web
- Tear-away stabilizer
- 1⅛ yards cotton crochet lace edging for dish towel and oven mitt
- Lace appliqués for crazy-patch hearts
- 1 package double-fold bias tape for pot holder (optional)
- Basic sewing supplies and equipment

If prequilted fabrics are not available, purchase additional fabric and batting. Layer and quilt by stitching squares through all layers.

Cutting
Note: *Enlarge patterns for pot holder, mitt front and mitt back 400 per cent.*
From solid fabric:
- Cut one 28 x 19-inch piece for dish towel.
- Cut one 12 x 14-inch piece for mitt band.

From quilted cotton fabric:
- Use pattern to cut one pot holder top.
- Use patterns to cut one mitt front and one mitt back.

From quilted Teflon fabric:
- Use pattern to cut one mitt pad.
- Use pattern to cut one pot holder bottom.

From print fabric:
- Cut one 2½ x 34-inch strip for pot holder bias binding. **Note:** *For added interest, cut strips from more than one print and piece them before binding pot holder.*
- Cut one 2 x 10-inch piece for loops on mitt and pot holder.
- Apply fusible web to scraps. Use patterns to cut one each A, B and C piece for each heart appliqué, mixing and matching fabrics as desired.

Appliqué
1. Sew heart pieces together.
2. Press seams open and stitch along each seam on the right side with a decorative stitch.
3. Stitch to object as instructed, using a satin stitch with 2–3mm-wide short stitch length. **Note:** *Pivot needle as needed on outer curves of the heart.*
4. Frame satin stitches with a decorative stitch.

Hanging Loop
1. Press 2 x 10-inch piece for loops in half, wrong sides together, with long edges matching.
2. Open strip and press long edges to centre fold. Stitch along both long edges.

3. Cut length in half to make two 5-inch lengths. Fold each length in half with ends together. Set loops aside.

Dish Towel Assembly

1. Narrow-hem all four sides of dish towel.

2. Sew crochet lace trim across lower edge.

3. Sew a decorative stitch across lower edge above lace trim.

4. Fuse heart appliqué in place. Stitch around outer raw edges (see Appliqué instructions, page 86).

Pot Holder

Note: Use ½-inch-wide seam allowance.

1. Fuse appliqué to pot holder top. Stitch around outer raw edges (see Appliqué instructions).

2. Pin ends of loop to pot holder top at upper corner with raw edges even.

3. Baste pot holder top and pot holder bottom with wrong sides together.

4. Finish edges with bias binding.

Oven Mitt

Note: Use ¼-inch-wide seam allowance unless otherwise stated.

1. Fuse appliqué to oven mitt front. Stitch around outer raw edges (see Appliqué instructions).

2. Pin ends of loop to mitt front as indicated on pattern, having raw edges even.

3. With right sides together and loop sandwiched between, sew both edges of mitt front and mitt back together between dots.

4. With right sides together, baste mitt pad to mitt front and mitt back. Machine-stitch around edges of mitt pad.

5. Baste crochet lace trim to one long edge of mitt band. Stitch short edges of mitt band together using ½-inch-wide seam allowance. Press seam.

6. Fold band in half with wrong sides together. Stitch raw edges of band to raw edges of mitt, making sure lace trim is next to outside of mitt.

7. Turn folded edge of band to inside of mitt and hand- or machine-stitch to seam line. ✦

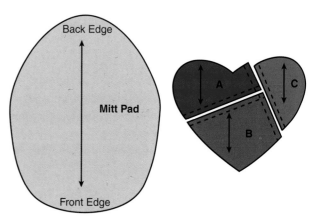

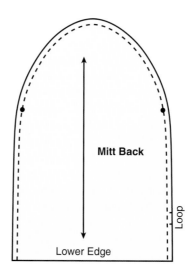

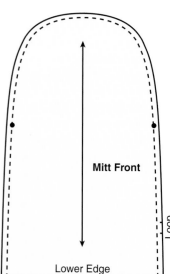

Romance in the Kitchen Patterns
Enlarge 400%

Dyeing for a Picnic

Candy-coloured table accessories will be a hit at your next picnic or tailgate party. Transform a wooden picnic basket from drab to dazzling with the application of cold-water dye. For the matching accessories, white cotton fabric was used and dyed in a variety of colours. Simple appliqué motifs are added to enhance the accessories. This set turns a picnic into a truly special event.

DESIGNS BY JANIS BULLIS

Skill Level
Intermediate

Finished Sizes
Blanket: 39 x 49 inches
Flatware Server: 10 x 17 inches, unfolded
Wine-Bottle Holder: 13 inches long
Placemat: 12 x 18 inches
Napkin: 13 x 13 inches

Materials
- 6 yards of white 44/45-inch-wide medium weight cotton fabric
- Nonwoven lightweight fusible interfacing
- Nonwoven medium to heavyweight fusible interfacing
- Paper-backed fusible web
- 2 yards of ⅞-inch ribbon
- Quilt batting
- Poster board
- Craft paper
- Staple gun and staples
- Cold-water fabric dyes (see sidebar on page 93): red, orange, green, blue, rose, coral, lilac, bright pink
- Water-soluble fabric pen
- Wooden picnic basket
- Cardboard
- All-purpose sewing threads to match colours of fabrics
- Basic sewing supplies and equipment

Instructions
Project Notes: *If the fabric you have chosen for appliqués is lightweight, support it with a lightweight fusible interfacing for added body. Be sure to apply the interfacing after the fabric has been dyed.*

Cut yardages into amounts given for individual projects and dye these (see Dyeing Fabric & Wood sidebar on page 93).

Use ½ inch for seam allowances.

Use matching threads for stitching unless otherwise stated.

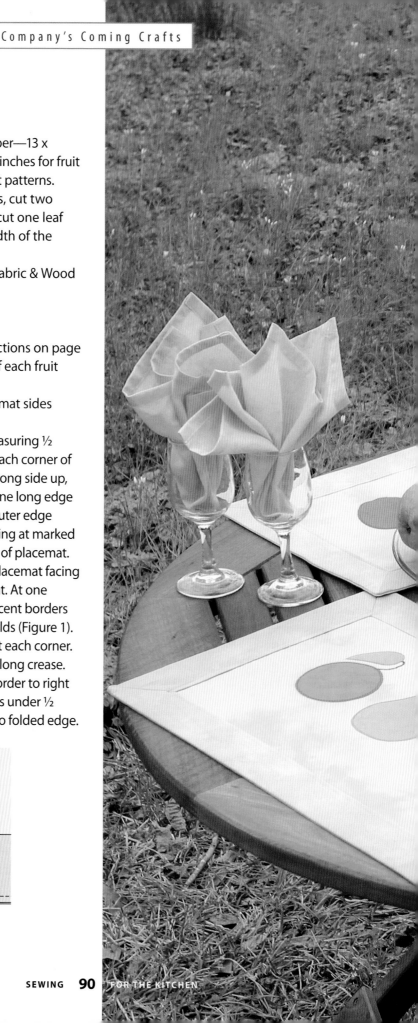

Placemat

Cutting & Fabric Preparation

- Draw the following patterns on paper—13 x 19 inches for placemat sides, 3 x 14 inches for fruit and 3 x 20 inches for leaves. Cut out patterns.
- From undyed fabric, using patterns, cut two placemat sides, three fruit pieces, cut one leaf piece and two 3-inch strips the width of the yardage for borders.
- Dye fabrics following the Dyeing Fabric & Wood instructions in sidebar on page 93.

Assembly

1. Following How to Appliqué instructions on page 8, cut, position, fuse and stitch one of each fruit design centre on one placemat side.

2. With wrong sides facing, pin placemat sides together.

3. For border with mitred corners, measuring ½ inch from each adjacent edge, mark each corner of the placemat back with a dot. With wrong side up, centre one long border piece across one long edge of placemat side. Stitch ½ inch from outer edge through all layers, beginning and ending at marked dots. Repeat for each remaining edge of placemat. Press seams open. With back side of placemat facing up, fold borders back against placemat. At one corner, fold back the ends of two adjacent borders to create a mitre from two diagonal folds (Figure 1). Press to crease folds. Repeat mitring at each corner. Stitch ends of border strips together along crease. Trim excess fabric from corner. Turn border to right side of placemat. Press. Turn raw edges under ½ inch and pin in place. Topstitch close to folded edge.

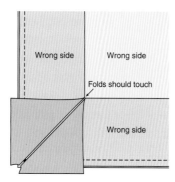

Figure 1

Blanket

Cutting & Fabric Preparation

- From undyed fabric, cut one piece 41 x 51 inches for blanket, cut three pieces each 6 inches square for fruit and leaf motifs, cut four 4-inch strips across the width of the yardage for borders.
- Dye fabrics following the Dyeing Fabric & Wood instructions in sidebar on facing page.

Assembly

1. Following How to Appliqué instructions on page 8, cut, position, fuse and stitch one of each fruit design at one corner on right side of blanket.
2. For border, work in same manner as border for placemat assembly.

Flatware Server

Cutting & Fabric Preparation

- Draw a rectangle 16 x 19 inches on paper. Using a saucer or small dinner plate, round off each corner of rectangle. Cut out pattern.
- From undyed fabric, using pattern, cut two side pieces, cut one piece 3 x 19 inches for decorative band.
- Dye fabrics following the Dyeing Fabric & Wood instructions in sidebar on facing page.
- From quilt batting, cut one piece according to pattern piece.

Assembly

1. Baste batting piece to wrong side of one side piece.
2. Turn under and press ½ inch on each long edge of decorative band piece. Measuring 4 inches from one long edge of batted side piece, topstitch band in place on right side. Cut two 18-inch ribbon pieces

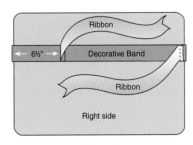

Figure 2

and tack one end of one ribbon to end of decorative band. Tack end of other ribbon 6½ inches from opposite end of decorative band (Figure 2).
3. Leaving an opening on top edge, stitch side pieces, right sides together, being careful not to catch loose ends of ribbons in seam. Clip curved edges. Turn right side out. Turn raw edges of opening to inside. Press.
4. Fold bottom edge of server piece up 4 inches to form pocket (Figure 3). Topstitch through all layers ¼ inch in around side and top edges.

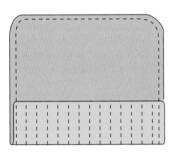

Figure 3

5. With outside of server facing you, mark lines at 1¼-inch intervals across pocket area of piece. Topstitch along each line, starting at edge of decorative band and ending at bottom of pocket.

Wine-Bottle Cover

Cutting & Fabric Preparation

- From undyed fabric, cut one piece 8 x 31 inches for cover, cut one piece 3 x 16 inches for top border.
- Dye fabrics following the Dyeing Fabric & Wood instructions in sidebar on facing page.

Assembly

1. On larger rectangle, on wrong side of fabric, measure 2 inches in from one short end and mark a dot in each seam line of each long edge. With right sides facing, fold rectangle in half crosswise. From dot to folded edge, stitch fabric together along each long edge. Clip seam allowance in to each dot. Press seams open and turn bottle cover right side out.
2. With wrong sides facing, complete each seam by stitching from the cut edge to the dot. Press seams open and turn to wrong side again.

3. Shape a paper bag bottom by folding a triangle in each corner (Figure 4), meeting the side seam to the bottom fold of the bag. At right angles to the side seam, stitch a 2-inch long seam through sides and bottom of bag.

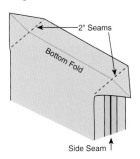

Figure 4

4. With right sides together, fold small rectangle in half crosswise and stitch short ends together. Press seam open. With right side of border facing wrong side of cover, pin and stitch border to open edge of cover matching one seam. Press seam open. Turn right side out. Turn border down over top of cover. Fold under ½ inch on lower edge of border and pin to cover. Topstitch border in place. Working 4

inches from top edge and centred between two seams, stitch centre of ribbon to cover.

Napkin

Cutting & Fabric Preparation
• From undyed fabric, cut one 16-inch-square piece for each napkin.
• Dye fabric pieces following the Dyeing Fabric & Wood instructions in sidebar.

Assembly
Press a ½-inch double-fold hem around raw edges of each napkin. Topstitch around hemmed edges.

Picnic Basket

Cutting & Fabric Preparation
• Using basket lid as a pattern, trace a pattern piece onto paper. Add ½ inch for seam allowance.
• From undyed fabric, using paper pattern, cut one piece for lid cover, cut three pieces each 6 inches square for fruit and leaf motifs.

Dyeing Fabric & Wood

Fabric dyeing is fun and now very easy to do with cold-water dyes. Coordinate your fabric and wood or wicker projects with the same colour dye. Dyeing wood is similar to staining and allows the beauty of the wood grain to show. For best results read thoroughly and follow the instructions available with the purchased dye package.

First weigh the fabric or determine the approximate weight of the item by studying the chart available in the dye package instructions. *Note: Take advantage of the fact that you will be dyeing the fabric before the item is made. Instead of working with the cut yardage, cut each piece of fabric to the approximate cutting size of the item to be made. Because so often shrinkage will occur, cut the fabric at least 6 inches wider and longer than the cutting dimensions of the project. Wash and rinse the fabric to remove all finishes before dyeing. Do not dry the fabric; leave it damp for the dyeing process.*

Mix the dye bath according to the package instructions adding table salt and the dye fixative accordingly. Immerse and stir the fabric for 10 minutes; then let the mixture sit, stirring occasionally, for 50 minutes. Rinse the fabric thoroughly; then wash the fabric once again. The result is a beautiful soft pastel or a vibrant bright colour according to your specifications.

Wood or wicker can be dipped into the dye bath or stained by applying the dye with a brush. Use unfinished wood or strip it of all paint, wax or finishes before dyeing.

Some of these picnic projects were given added interest by loosely tying the fabric pieces, then dyeing them to achieve a marbleized effect. If the fabric is bound tightly with rubber bands in sequential order, you can produce a tie-dyed look.

- Trim seam allowance from pattern piece. From plywood and cardboard, cut one piece each according to pattern piece.
- Dye fabric pieces following the Dyeing Fabric & Wood instructions in sidebar on page 93.

Dyeing Basket
See Dyeing Fabric & Wood instructions on page 93.

Padded Lid Assembly
1. Following How to Appliqué instructions on page 8, cut, position, fuse and stitch one of each fruit design on centre of lid cover piece.

2. Using a zigzag stitch or serger, clean finish the raw edge of lid cover piece.

3. Using a long machine basting stitch and a heavier button and carpet thread, stitch a row of gathering stitches ¼ inch from edge of lid cover.

4. Place batting on top of basket lid. Position fabric lid cover over batting and pull gathering thread to wrap edges of fabric to underside of lid. Staple edges in place, beginning at centre of the straight edges and making your way to the gathered corners.

5. Cover raw edges of fabric by stapling cardboard piece to underside of lid. ◆

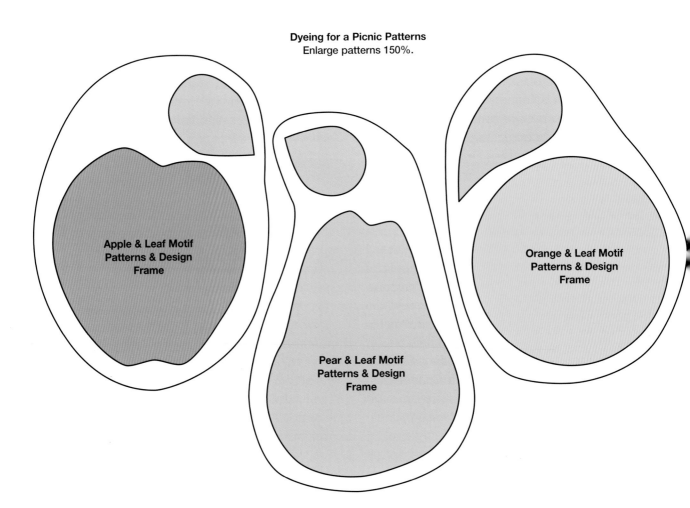

Dyeing for a Picnic Patterns
Enlarge patterns 150%.

Apple & Leaf Motif
Patterns & Design
Frame

Pear & Leaf Motif
Patterns & Design
Frame

Orange & Leaf Motif
Patterns & Design
Frame

A Tisket, a Tasket, Make a Bread Basket

Low-sew projects are always fun, and this batik bread basket is a winner. Make a few for gift-giving or some for different holidays. Storage isn't a problem because the basket will store flat.

DESIGN BY PAULINE RICHARDS

Skill Level
Beginner

Finished Size
Approximately 10 x 2½ inches

Materials
- ½ yard batik fabric
- 15 x 15-inch sheet double-sided fusible, heavy craft interfacing
- ⅜-inch-wide water-soluble double-sided adhesive tape
- 6 Chinese ball buttons with loops
- Teflon press cloth
- Basic sewing supplies and equipment

Instructions
1. Using patterns provided, cut one base and six sides from interfacing.
2. Place batik fabric right side down on ironing surface. Place interfacing pieces on wrong side of fabric as shown in Figure 1, allowing ⅛ inch between sides and base. Cover with Teflon press cloth and press pieces to fabric.

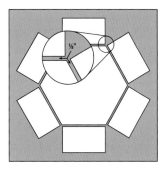

Figure 1

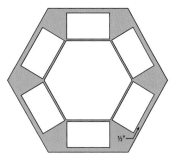

Figure 2

3. Trim around pieces as shown in Figure 2, allowing ½ inch seam allowance on outer edge.
4. Using cut-out hexagon shape as a pattern; cut another piece from fabric for basket lining.

5. On basket, fold ½-inch seam allowance to inside and press with iron (Figure 3).

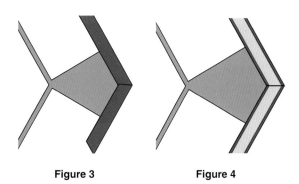

Figure 3   Figure 4

6. Adhere fusible adhesive tape to seam allowance following manufacturer's instructions (Figure 4). **Note:** *Tape should be approximately ⅛ inch from folded edge.*

7. Position Chinese ball buttons and loops around edge of basket as shown in Figure 5 and press onto adhesive tape.

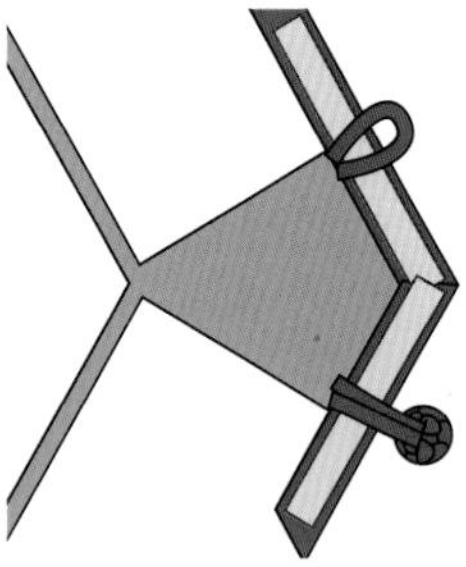

Figure 5

8. Carefully position basket lining inside basket, matching edges. Fold ½-inch seam allowance to inside and finger-press in place so edges of lining are even with basket edges.

9. Thoroughly press to secure basket lining to basket. Straight-stitch around basket ⅛ inch from edge.

10. With fingernail, define stitching lines between each side piece and between sides and bottom; mark lines with chalk (Figure 6). Straight-stitch on marked lines.

Figure 6

11. Fold sides of basket up, and slip loops over buttons to secure. ◆

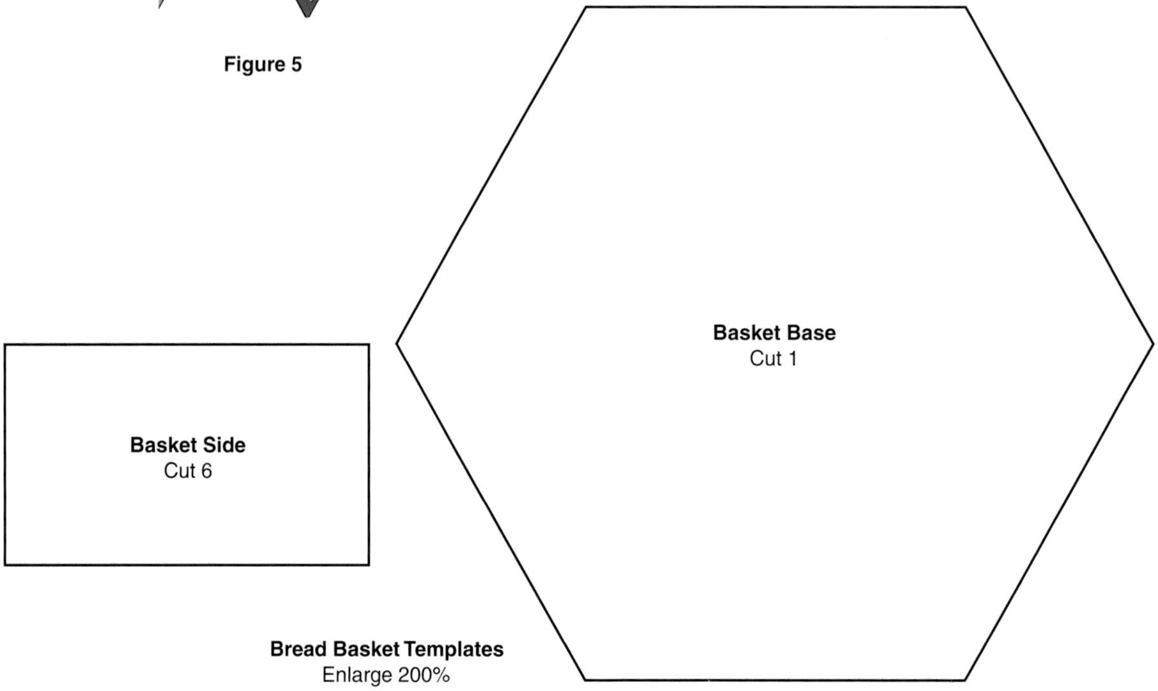

Basket Side
Cut 6

Basket Base
Cut 1

Bread Basket Templates
Enlarge 200%

Store & Serve Plate Caddies

Store your dishes in style with protective cases.

DESIGNS BY CAROL ZENTGRAF

Skill Level
Beginner

Finished Sizes
Dinner Plate Caddy: 12 x 5 inches
Salad Plate Caddy: 10 x 5 inches

Materials for Each Caddy
- ⅔ yard 45-inch-wide double-face quilted cotton fabric
- 4½ yards coordinating double-fold bias tape
- 1⅛ yards ¾-inch-wide sew-on hook-and-loop tape
- Permanent fabric adhesive
- Basic sewing supplies and equipment

Cutting for Dinner Plate Caddy
From double-face quilted fabric:
- Cut two 12-inch-diameter circles for top and bottom.
- Cut one 39 x 6-inch strip for bottom side.
- Cut one 39 x 2-inch strip for top side.

Cutting for Salad Plate Caddy
From double-face quilted fabric:
- Cut two 10-inch-diameter circles for top and bottom.
- Cut one 32 x 6-inch strip for bottom side.
- Cut one 32 x 2-inch strip for top side.

Assembly
Notes: *Serge seams, or stitch using a scant ¼-inch-wide seam allowance and finish seams with a zigzag stitch.*
1. Stitch short edges of bottom side piece together with inner sides together. Cover seam with bias tape (Figure 1). Repeat for top side piece.

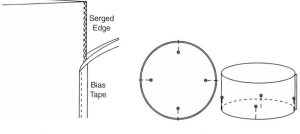

Figure 1   Figure 2

2. Fold each side piece in fourths and mark folds with pins. Fold top and bottom pieces in fourths and mark in same manner (Figure 2).
3. Open pieces and pin top and top side, inner sides together, matching quarter marks and easing sides to fit. Pin bottom and bottom side together in same manner. Stitch together and bind seams.
4. Finish raw edges of top and bottom sides; bind with bias tape.
5. On outside of bottom side, use chalk wheel to mark a line 1¾ inches from upper edge of side.
6. Pin the loop side of hook-and-loop tape around sides, aligning upper edge of tape with chalk line. Stitch both edges of tape to side using thread to match inner fabric.
7. Using permanent fabric adhesive, glue hook side of hook-and-loop tape to inside lower edge of top side; let dry thoroughly.
8. To use for storage, stack plates in caddy up to 5 inches high. Fold upper edge of side over plates and attach lid using hook-and-loop tape. To use for serving, remove the lid and fold over the top edge of bottom side to conceal the hook-and-loop tape. ◆

Casserole Carrier

Enclose a baking dish and give as a gift.

DESIGN BY BETH WHEELER

Skill Level
Beginner

Finished Size
Casserole Carrier: Approximately 12-inch diameter for 1½-quart covered casserole
Note: *To change casserole cover size, measure covered casserole (Figure 1) and add 2 inches. Cut cover using new center diameter.*

Materials
- 26-inch squares of 2 coordinating 100 per cent cotton fabrics
- 26-inch square fusible fleece or old ironing board cover
- 26-inch square insulated fleece or batting (has a shiny metallic finish on one side)
- 2 yards cotton cord
- 1 package contrasting maxi piping
- Basic sewing supplies and equipment

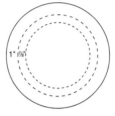

Figure 1

Instructions
1. Cut a 26-inch circle of each cotton fabric. Cut a 25-inch circle of fusible fleece and insulated fleece.
2. Centre and bond fusible-fleece circle to wrong side of one fabric circle, following manufacturer's directions. This will be the outer shell. Stitch piping around the periphery.
3. Centre insulated fleece on wrong side of remaining fabric circle with shiny side toward fabric; baste in place around periphery.
4. Draw a line 1 inch away from periphery of bonded circle with chalk marker. Draw another line ⅞ inch away from first line as shown in Figure 2.

Work two ⅝-inch buttonholes inside those lines, as shown in Figure 3.

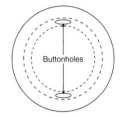

Figure 2   Figure 3

5. Place backed fabric circles together, right sides facing. Stitch around the periphery with a ½-inch seam allowance, leaving an opening for turning.
6. Clip curves; turn right side out. Close opening with a hand-sewing needle and thread.
7. Stitch along chalk lines through all layers to create a casing.
8. Cut cotton cord in half. Feed one piece through one buttonhole, around the casing and back out through the same buttonhole, as in Figure 4. Tie ends of cord together in a knot. Feed remaining cord through other buttonhole, around casing and back out through the same buttonhole. Tie ends of cord together in a knot.

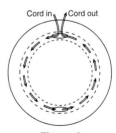

Figure 4

9. Place covered casserole inside carrier; pull knotted ends of cords to fit the carrier around the casserole. ◆

Pillow Trio

Here are tips for successful pillows in three wonderful styles. Learn the basics of ruffles, shirred cord and flange styles which coordinate in charming spring colours. The techniques you learn here can be applied to any fabric and pillow size.

DESIGNS BY JANIS BULLIS

Skill Level
Beginner

A Trio of Pillows With Creative Finishes

Three beautifully coordinated fabrics are used to change ordinary pillows into creative works of art. The colours and styles used in the printed fabrics resemble a beautiful watercolour painting. Solid-colour coordinates are used to accent the print and help to frame each painting. Each pillow features its own interesting top treatment and creative edge finish. The sailboat print shows outline quilting with a quilt batting lining and helps add dimension to the design. It also shows not one, but two custom-made ruffles. One ruffle is an eyelet trim, and the second is a bias-cut ruffle of double thickness. Both are gathered to a generous 2½ times the fullness.

Fusible interfacing and fusible web come to your aid when attaching a pucker-free satin stitch appliqué. A matching shirred cord accents the perimeter of this pillow. The third pillow illustrates a foolproof, step-by-step guide for making an applied flange. Using a covered-button kit allows the centre buttons to match the framed flange perfectly.

Tools You Will Need for All Three Pillows
- Sewing machine
- Iron and ironing board
- Dressmaker shears
- Water or air-soluble fabric-marking pen
- Tissue paper
- Pencil
- Yardstick

Quilted Sailboats Pillow With Ruffle

Watercolour sailboats are outlined and quilted through a double layer of quilt batting to provide increased dimension. The pillow top is then framed with two rows of ruffles. The first ruffle is flat eyelet trimming which has been generously gathered to 2½ times the fullness. The second ruffle is constructed from a wide bias strip of fabric and also shows a generous fullness that mimics the look of a custom-made decorator pillow.

Materials

- 2¼ yards of 54-inch-wide decorator fabric
- 5 yards of 2½-inch-wide flat eyelet trim
- 18-inch pillow form
- Two 19-inch squares of cotton quilt batting
- All-purpose sewing thread in two colours
- Hand-sewing needle
- Heavy-duty thread in neutral colour

Cutting

Notes: This pillow measures 18 inches square when finished plus a 2-inch-wide eyelet trim and 3-inch-wide lined self ruffle on all edges. The fabric cutting dimensions for this pillow includes ½-inch seam allowances.

- Using tissue paper, pencil and yardstick, measure and cut a paper pattern 19 inches x 19 inches. Use a T-square or the adjacent edges of a large book to draw perfect right angles at each corner.
- Using paper pattern, cut two pieces from quilt batting. Using paper pattern, cut a pillow front and back from decorator fabric. ***Note:*** *For pillow front, be sure to position paper on centre of most prominent fabric design motif (sailboats). Also, position paper pattern so it will not interfere with cutting bias strips in the next step.*

- Following the instructions for Making Bias Strips (page 8), cut four bias strips from fabric measuring exactly 7 inches wide and approximately 45 inches long. Stitch strips together to form a continuous strip as indicated in instructions.

Assembly

1. With all edges even, position two layers of quilt batting under pillow top with right side up. Pin all layers together along all four edges. Using large basting stitches, stitch six or eight rows of hand stitches through all three layers.

2. At the sewing machine, using matching or contrasting thread, stitch along all edges of the printed motif, following straight lines, curves and pivoting at the corners. Backstitch at the beginning and end of each row of stitching or bring the threads to the wrong side of the fabric and tie off in a knot. Stitch as much or as little of the detail of the motif as you like. Once complete, clip and remove the large basting stitches. Cutting close to the stitches, clip away one layer of quilt batting from all edges of the largest motifs, allowing these motifs to have more dimension and stand out more prominently.

3. With the wrong sides facing, fold the continuous bias strip in half lengthwise; do not press. Pin cut edges together periodically along the entire strip. Notice how the strip is made from four sections of fabric somewhat equal in length. At the point of one of the four seams in the bias strip, position the cut edges of the folded bias strip under the presser foot on the ¼-inch seam mark on the throat plate (along the inside of the presser foot). Cut four pieces of heavy-duty thread, each approximately 72 inches (two yards) long.

Note: *Lightweight string or even dental floss substitutes nicely for heavy-duty thread.*

4. At one end, position the string under the centre of the presser foot and on top of the fabric. Set the sewing machine dials to a medium width but very long zigzag stitch. Beginning and ending at each of the four seams in the bias strip, zigzag over each of the strings. Use four lengths of string for four sections of bias strip. Do not catch the string in your stitches; adjust the length or width of the stitch if you need to (Figure 1).

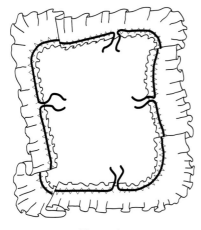

Figure 1

5. Pulling periodically from both ends of each string, push the fabric along the string until each of the four sections gather to measure approximately 18 inches.

6. With right sides facing, stitch together the short ends of the eyelet trim. Using soluble pen, measure and mark the trim into four equal lengths. Following the above directions, stitch ¼ inch from the long cut edge, zigzagging over four lengths of string between each of the four sections of trim. Gather up the trim to measure approximately 18 inches to a section.

7. On the right side of the pillow top, mark the centre at each of the four edges on the fabric. Begin with the eyelet trim. With right sides of trim to right side of fabric and cut edges even, pin each of the four marked divisions (the string ends) to the marked centres of the pillow top. Distributing the fullness of the trim evenly, continue pinning the trim along all edges of the pillow top using plenty of pins.

Note: *Push a little extra fullness into the corners of the pillow and a little less along the straight edges.*

8. Following a ¼-inch seam allowance, machine-baste the eyelet to the pillow top. Next use the fabric ruffle. With ruffle facing wrong side of the trim and all cut edges even, pin each of the four seamed divisions (the string ends) to the marked centres of the pillow top. Distributing the fullness of the ruffle evenly, continue pinning the ruffle along all edges of the pillow top using plenty of pins.

9. Following a ⅜-inch seam allowance, machine-baste the ruffle to the eyelet and the pillow top.

10. With right sides of fabric facing, pin the pillow back to the pillow top along all edges with the eyelet trim and ruffle sandwiched in between. Following a ½-inch seam allowance and stitching through many layers, machine-stitch the pillow back to the pillow top, leaving an approximate 12-inch opening along the centre of one edge.

11. Clip corners of seam allowance up to stitching. Turn pillow to the right side. Insert pillow form through opening. Using hand stitches, slipstitch opening closed.

Appliquéd Pillow With Shirred Cord

A solid-colour coordinate is cut from the pattern provided and applied to a flowery pillow top using a pucker-free appliqué method. The same fabric is used to make a bias-cut shirred cord which outlines the perimeter of the pillow. For an authentic "throw" pillow, purchase twice as much interfacing and web, and appliqué a flower on both the front and back.

Materials
- ⅝ yard of 54-inch-wide print decorator fabric
- 1½ yards of 54-inch-wide solid decorator fabric
- 20-inch pillow form
- 2½ yards of ¹²⁄₃₂-inch (⅜ inch to ⅝ inch) cotton filler cord
- One piece each medium to heavyweight fusible interfacing: 4 x 4 inches, 14 x 14 inches
- One piece each paper-backed fusible web: 4 x 4 inches, 14 x 14 inches
- All-purpose sewing thread in two colours
- Hand sewing needle
- Heavy-duty sewing thread in neutral colour
- Decorative sewing thread in two colours for application of flower (optional)
- Sewing bodkin or large safety pin
- 2 safety pins

Cutting

Notes: *This pillow measures 20 inches when finished with a ½-inch-wide finished shirred cord on all edges. The fabric cutting dimensions for this pillow include ¾-inch-wide seam allowances for easy handling and less twisting of the shirred cord.*

- Using tissue paper, pencil and yardstick, measure and cut a paper pattern 21½ x 21½ inches. Use a T-square or the adjacent edges of a large book to draw perfect right angles at each corner.
- Using paper pattern, cut a pillow front and back from print decorator fabric.
- Following the instructions for Making Bias Strips (page 8), cut four bias strips from fabric measuring exactly 3 inches wide and approximately 50 inches long. Stitch strips together to form a continuous strip as indicated in instructions.
- Cut a 4-inch square from the printed fabric and a 14-inch square from the solid-colour fabric. Following the interfacing and web manufacturer's instructions and matching like-sized squares, fuse the interfacing to the wrong side of the fabric squares. Fuse the web to the interfaced side of the fabric squares. Using the flower petal and flower centre pattern, trace the design on the paper backing of the fusible web and cut through all layers. Remove the paper backing from the petal and the centre. Position the two flower pieces on the centre of the pillow top and fuse into place.

Assembly

1. Set a zigzag (satin) stitch on your sewing machine with a very short length and a medium to wide width. Relax the upper tension to the buttonhole indication if you have one. Attach the appliqué or decorative stitch foot. Select a matching-colour standard or decorative thread. With slow and steady movements, stitch the appliqué to the pillow allowing the left swing of the needle to penetrate the appliqué and the right swing of the needle to jump off the appliqué and onto the pillow top alone. Stitch the edges of the flower petal and the flower centre, encasing the edges of the fabric. For best results, practice first on a few scraps of fabric set up with interfacing and web to mimic your pillow top.

2. With the wrong sides facing, fold the continuous bias strip in half lengthwise; do not press. Pin the cut edges together periodically along the entire strip. Stitch the two layers together, down the centre of the folded strip, ¾ inch from the cut edges and ¾ inch from the folded edge. Leave a break in the stitches about 6 inches long to either side of one of the joining seams.

3. Measure and cut the filler cord exactly 86 inches long. Using the soluble pen, mark the filler cord 3 inches from each end, leaving 80 inches in the centre. Attach a bodkin or large safety pin to one end of the cord and feed it through the tunnel in the bias strip. Pull on the cord and push the fabric along the cord to gather. Pin a safety pin through the cord and fabric at each end of the fabric opening to keep the cord from slipping out (Figure 2). Distribute the fabric fullness evenly along the cord.

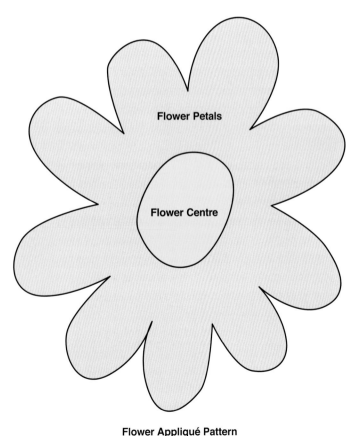

Flower Petals

Flower Centre

Flower Appliqué Pattern
Enlarge Pattern 200%

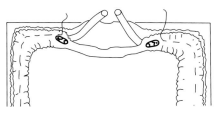

Figure 2

4. On the right side of the pillow top, mark the four centres of each of the four edges of fabric. On the right side of the pillow top with all cut edges even, pin the shirred cord to all edges of the pillow top. Begin by matching each of the four seamed divisions of the strip to the marked centres of the pillow top. Distributing the fullness of the cord evenly, continue pinning the cord along all edges of the pillow top using plenty of pins.

Note: Push a little extra fullness into the corners of the pillow and a little less along the straight edges.

5. When most of the shirred cord is pinned to the pillow top, join the filler cord ends by trimming the excess and butt-joining with glue or hand stitches. With your fingers and more pins, gather the fabric around the join to resemble the rest of the shirred cord. Following a ¾-inch seam allowance, machine-baste the entire shirred cord to the pillow top.

6. With right sides of fabric facing, pin the pillow back to the pillow top along all edges with the shirred cord sandwiched in between. Following a ¾-inch seam allowance and stitching through all layers, machine-stitch the pillow back to the pillow top, leaving an approximate 12-inch opening along the centre of one edge.

7. Trim seam allowance. Clip corners of seam allowance up to stitching. Turn pillow to the right side. Insert pillow form through opening. Using hand stitches, slipstitch opening closed.

Centre Button Pillow
With Foolproof Flange

Geometrics are the featured story here with a plain 16-inch pillow that grows to a 21-inch tailored work of art. The pillow shows circular buttons on a square pillow with a rectangular flange framing a polka-dot print. The step-by-step instructions for accurate measuring and cutting make this applied flange foolproof.

Materials
- ½ yard of 54-inch-wide print decorator fabric
- ½ yard of 54-inch-wide solid decorator fabric
- 16-inch pillow form
- Covered-button kit with 2 (1⅛-inch) buttons
- All-purpose sewing thread in two colours
- Hand sewing needle
- Heavy-duty thread in neutral colour
- Large-eyed hand needle

Cutting
Notes: This pillow measures 16 inches square when finished plus a 2½-inch-wide finished flange on all edges. The fabric cutting dimensions for this pillow includes ½-inch seam allowances.

- Using tissue paper, pencil and yardstick, measure and cut a paper pattern 17 x 17 inches for pillow front and back. Also measure and cut a paper pattern 3½ x 22 inches for flange. Use a T-square or the adjacent edges of a large book to draw perfect right angles at each corner.
- Using paper pillow pattern, cut a pillow front and back from print decorator fabric. Using paper flange pattern, cut eight flanges from solid-colour fabric. Measure and cut accurately.

Assembly
1. Using the soluble pen and working on the wrong side of the fabric of each flange, measure and mark two dots ½ inch in from one long edge and 3 inches in from each short end. Draw two diagonal lines, each from the marked dot to the corner on the opposite long edge of the flange.

2. Referring to Figure 3, with right sides of fabric facing, short ends of two flanges even and diagonal lines aligned, pin together two flanges at each of the four corners along marked diagonals to create a square frame. On each corner, stitch two layers of fabric together from the dot to the corner along marked diagonal lines, backstitching at each end. Trim off triangle shaped scrap of fabric measuring approximately ¼ inch from stitching. Press seam open. Repeat for four corners of remaining four flanges to yield two identical mitred-corner picture frames.

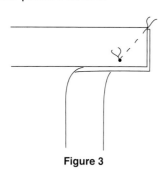

Figure 3

3. Using soluble pen on the right side of the pillow front, mark a dot on each corner, measuring ½ inch in from each edge. With right sides of fabric facing and cut edges even, pin the inside edge of one picture frame flange assembly to the outside edge of the pillow front—the stitched mitred corner of the flange should match up to each marked dot of the pillow. Stitch through both layers ½ inch from the cut edge, beginning and ending (backstitching) at each dot in each corner (Figure 4).

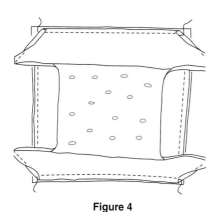

Figure 4

Note: *Do not pin all four edges at once. Pin and stitch two opposite edges; then pin and stitch remaining opposite edges.*

4. Repeat for remaining picture-frame flange and pillow back. When all seams are complete, first press open each seam, then press seam allowances towards outer edges.

5. With right sides of fabric facing, pin together all edges of pillow top assembly to pillow back assembly, matching corner seams and cut edges. Stitch through both layers on all four edges, pivoting in the mitred seams at each corner and leaving a 10-inch break in the stitching near the centre on one of the four sides. Backstitch securely at each end of the opening. Clip away seam allowance at each corner; press all the seams open.

Note: *Insert a pressing ham, sleeve roll or small rolled towel inside the pillow through the opening to simplify pressing open seams. Turn assembly to right side. Press edges flat, turning in both seam allowances in opening area.*

6. Pin pillow top to pillow back along all inner seams where they meet the flanges.

Note: *Position the pins on the printed fabric parallel to the seam, turning the pillow top up, then bottom up, then top up again making sure the two seams are aligned on top of each other.*

7. Using a zipper foot, topstitch through both layers on the printed fabrics very close to the seam and solid-colour flange fabric—stitch all four edges, leaving a 10-inch opening just above the same location as the 10-inch opening already in the assembly. Backstitch securely at each end of the opening.

8. Insert pillow form into assembly. Align and pin seams, then topstitch inside opening closed using a hand backstitch that mimics a machine stitch. Also by hand, slipstitch outside opening closed along folded seam allowance.

9. Following the kit manufacturer's directions, cover two buttons with solid-colour fabric and using heavy-duty thread and needle, stitch buttons to centres of pillow. ◆

Raggedy Taggedy

No tedious clipping allowed with these rugged pillows reminiscent of raggedy-edge quilts. Bias-cut strips of sturdy denim and inside-out seaming plus a toss in the wash make the pillow covers "bloom."

DESIGNS BY CAROL MOFFATT

Skill Level
Beginner

Finished Sizes
Make It Monotone: 24 inches square
Denim Checkerboard: 18 inches square

Make It Monotone

Materials
- 3½ yards 54/60-inch-wide light blue denim
- All-purpose thread to match fabric
- 24-inch-square knife-edge pillow form
- Rotary cutter, mat and ruler with 45-degree-angle line
- Basic sewing tools and equipment

Cutting
- Wash and press the denim.
- Fold the fabric in half lengthwise with selvages aligned, and make sure the fold is lying flat and smooth.
- Place the fabric on the cutting mat with the folded edge closest to you.
- Beginning at the lower left-hand corner of the folded fabric, position the 45-degree-angle line parallel to the fabric fold and make the first bias cut (Figure 1).
- Continue cutting the fabric on the bias, spacing

the cuts 4 inches apart across the entire piece of folded fabric. Leave the strips layered and treat each layered set as a unit during the construction. Set aside the short strips for another project. You will use only the full-length double-layer bias strips that run from selvage to fold (Figure 2).

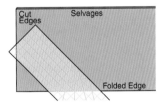

Figure 1

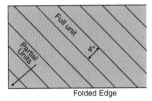

Figure 2

- Square off the angled ends of each double-layer strip (Figure 3).

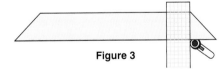

Figure 3

Assembly
Note: *Use ½-inch-wide seam allowances throughout.*

1. Sew the double-layered strips together in pairs (Figure 4).

2. Sew four pairs together for the pillow front. Repeat for the pillow back. Place one completed unit on the cutting mat

Figure 4

with the seam allowances on top. Cut the piece into 4-inch-wide strips. You should have eight strips. Repeat with the remaining pieced unit (Figure 5).

Figure 5

3. Sew eight strips together for the pillow front and repeat with the remaining strips for the pillow back. Alternate the seam-allowance direction at each intersection and pin in place before sewing (Figure 6).

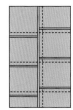

Figure 6

4. With the patchwork seam allowances on the outside, pin the pillow front and back together. Alternate the seam-allowance directions as you did when sewing the patchwork strips together. Machine-stitch ½ inch from three raw edges, backstitching at the beginning and end of the stitching. Machine-baste the remaining edges together.
5. Wash the pillow cover in the washing machine and dry in the dryer to make the raw-edge seam allowances "bloom."
6. Remove the basting and insert the pillow form. Pin the edges together and stitch, pushing the pillow form out of the way and using a zipper foot if necessary to complete the seam. If you prefer, you can hand-sew the last seam using a close backstitch.

Denim Checkerboard

Materials
- 54/60-inch-wide 100 per cent cotton denim
  1 yard light blue
  1 yard dark blue

- 18-inch-square knife-edge pillow form
- All-purpose thread to match fabrics
- Rotary cutter, mat and ruler with 45-degree-angle line
- Basic sewing supplies and equipment

Cutting
- Prepare each piece of fabric and then fold and cut into double-layer strips as directed in Cutting for Make It Monotone (Figures 1 and 2 on page 109). You will need six light denim double-layer strips and six dark denim double-layer strips.
- Square off the ends of the strips as shown in Figure 3 on page 109.

Assembly
Note: *Use ½-inch-wide seam allowances throughout.*
1. Pin and sew a light denim double-layer bias strip to each dark denim double-layer bias strip. Sew three of these units together for the pillow front and three for the pillow back (Figure 7). Cut each panel into six 4-inch-wide strips.

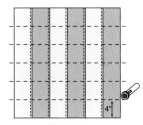

Figure 7

2. Arrange the strips checkerboard fashion and pin together with seam allowances alternating at each intersection as shown in Figure 6. Stitch (Figure 8).

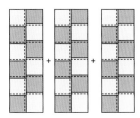

Figure 8

3. Complete the pillow following steps 4–6 for Make It Monotone (page 109). ✦

Eight Is Enough

Eight is enough for any pillow or cushion—eight corners that is! This fun shape is deceptively simple to sew. Just cut two squares and follow the steps below. Try combining two different fabrics for a different look. Two large buttons make this a tufted cushion. Tassels are optional.

DESIGN BY BARBARA WEILAND

Skill Level
Beginner

Finished Size
15 inches across, point to point

Materials
- 2 (17-inch) squares decorator fabric
- 2 large shank-style buttons, at least 1 inch in diameter
- All-purpose thread to match fabric
- Approximately 14 ounces polyester fibrefill
- Chopstick
- Air-soluble marking pen
- Long, large-eyed upholstery needle
- Gimp or polyester buttonhole twist or carpet thread
- Basic sewing tools and equipment

Assembly
Note: *Use ½-inch-wide seam allowances throughout.*
1. Machine-baste ½ inch from all four edges of each square. Fold each square in half and then in half again, and make ⅛-inch-long snips at the folds to mark the centre of each edge. Unfold (Figure 1).

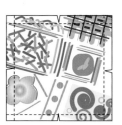
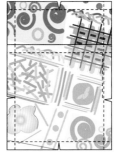

Figure 1   Figure 2

2. With right sides together, position one square on top of the other with the seam line at the corner of the top square at a snip mark on the bottom square. Align the snip mark on the top square with the seam line at the lower corner of the bottom square. Stitch from the seam line on the top square to the seam line on the bottom square. Backstitch carefully at the beginning and end of the seam. Make sure that the stitches do not pass the seam lines, and then carefully clip to, but not past, the stitching at the end of the short seam (Figure 2). Remove from the machine.
3. Turn the piece over and then pin and stitch the next side of the top square to the bottom square, matching snips and seam lines as for the first seam (Figure 3).

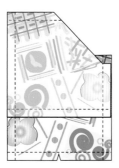

Figure 3

7. On the top and bottom of the eight-cornered pillow, measure and mark the centre with an air-soluble marking pen.

8. Cut an 18-inch-long piece of gimp, carpet thread or buttonhole twist and slip it through the shank of one button. Tie the threads in a secure knot (Figure 4).

Figure 4

4. Continue in this manner until you reach the last seam. Stitch only a few inches at the beginning and end of the last seam to leave a 6-inch opening in the centre.

5. Turn the cushion cover right side out. Turn under the seam allowance on one of the opening edges; press. Firmly stuff the cushion with polyester fibrefill, working it into each of the eight corners first. Use the chopstick to poke it into the corners.

6. When the pillow is completely stuffed, use doubled thread to invisibly sew the opening edges together with tiny slipstitches.

9. Thread one end of the thread into the upholstery needle. Centre the button on one side of the cushion and draw the needle through to the other side of the cushion. Remove the needle and repeat with the remaining thread end so that both ends are on the opposite side close to the centre mark.

10. Pull the thread ends through the shank of the remaining button from opposite directions, and then pull them tightly to compact the centre of the cushion as desired. Knot the thread ends securely under the button. ◆

Pillow Play!

- Experiment with this shape using different fabrics and trims.
- Try this pillow in smaller or larger sizes—just change the size of the square.
- Try using squares cut from two different fabrics for an interesting effect. Try a napped fabric like velveteen to create shaded variations as you turn the corners.
- Sew contrast piping to one of the two squares before assembling the cover so the seam lines have a strong outline.
- Add a tassel to each of the four corners on the top of the finished pillow. Securely and invisibly sew them in place. Tuck and tack the loops behind the tassel heads.

Stripe It Rich Pillow Duo

Make these two decorator pillows to discover the fun of working with stripes. It's easy to achieve two different looks with the same fabric by creating mitred designs.

DESIGNS BY CAROL ZENTGRAF

Skill Level
Beginner

Finished Sizes
Stripes Go Square Pillow: 14 inches square, excluding trim
All Points to Centre Pillow: 18 inches square, excluding trim

Materials
Stripes Go Square Pillow
- 1 yard 54-inch-wide striped decorator fabric
- 1⅝ yards sew-in brush fringe
- 14-inch square pillow form
- Repositionable ½-inch-wide fusible web
- Permanent fabric adhesive
- Pattern-tracing cloth or pattern paper
- All-purpose thread to match fabrics
- Rotary cutter, mat and ruler
- Basic sewing supplies and equipment

All Points to Centre Pillow
- 1⅓ yards 54-inch-wide striped decorator fabric
- 2⅛ yards tassel fringe with decorative header
- 18-inch-square pillow form
- Pattern-tracing cloth or pattern paper
- All-purpose thread to match fabrics
- Repositionable ½-inch-wide fusible web
- Permanent fabric adhesive

- Rotary cutter, mat and ruler
- Basic sewing supplies and equipment

Stripes Go Square Pillow

Note: *Use ½-inch-wide seam allowances throughout.*
1. Draw a 15-inch square on pattern tracing cloth or paper. Divide the square in half twice diagonally. Add ½-inch-wide seam allowances to all edges of one of the triangles. Cut out the triangle with the seam allowances to use for your pattern (Figure 1).

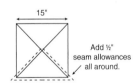

Figure 1

2. Place the pattern on the striped fabric with the base of the triangle parallel to the stripes. Cut the first triangle. Use it as a guide to cut a total of eight identical triangles (four for the front and four for the back).
3. Sew triangles together in pairs to make four identical triangles with perfectly matched stripes (see the sidebar on page 116). Press the seams open.
4. Sew two large triangles together along the long edge to create a square. Use the fusible web method in the sidebar to ensure a perfect match (Figure 2). Repeat for the pillow back.

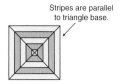

Stripes are parallel to triangle base.

Figure 2

5. With right sides together, baste the heading of the brush fringe to the outer edge of one pillow square, overlapping the ends neatly. The loops of the fringe should point to the centre of the pillow square.
6. With right sides together, sew the pillow back to the pillow front, leaving a 6-inch-long opening in one side. Clip across the corners and turn the pillow cover right side out. Press, turning under the seam allowances at the opening.
7. Insert the pillow form and slipstitch the opening closed.

All Points to Centre Pillow

Note: Use ½-inch-wide seam allowances throughout.
1. Draw a 19-inch square on pattern tracing cloth or paper. Add seam allowances and cut out as directed in Step 1 for the Stripes Go Square Pillow.
2. Place the pattern on the fabric with the triangle base perpendicular to the stripes and cut the first triangle. Use it as a guide to cut a total of eight identical triangles.
3. Sew the triangles together in pairs with stripes matching perfectly (see the sidebar) to make four large triangles. Press the seams open.
4. Sew the resulting triangles together in pairs and press the seams open. Take care to match the stripes at the seam line using the same fusible-tape method (Figure 3).

Figure 3

5. Sew the pillow front to the back ½ inch from all edges, leaving a 6-inch-long opening for turning in one side. Clip the seam allowances at each corner and turn the pillow cover right side out. Press, turning under the seam allowances at the opening.
6. Beginning at the centre of one edge, use permanent fabric adhesive to glue the trim in place along the pillow edges and create a neatly turned overlap at the point where the ends join.
7. Insert the pillow form and slipstitch the opening closed. ◆

Mitre Perfect!

1. To match the stripes perfectly, machine-baste ½ inch from the edge of one triangle. Apply repositionable sticky-back fusible web along the stitching in the seam allowance (Figure 4).

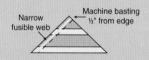

Narrow fusible web

Machine basting ½" from edge

Figure 4

2. Position a second triangle face down on the first triangle aligning the edges to be joined. Finger-press the taped edges together. Carefully lift the top fabric layer to make certain the stripes are aligned. Adjust if necessary.
3. When you are sure the layers are positioned for a perfect match, fuse in place following the manufacturer's directions. Stitch ½ inch from the raw edges and remove any basting that shows. Press the seam allowances to one side. **Note:** *You can adapt this technique, using double-sided basting tape if you prefer not to fuse the seams together.*

Rolled, Tailored & Tied

Snuggle up with a linen neck-roll pillow with synthetic suede piping, binding and ties.

DESIGN BY CAROL ZENTGRAF

Skill Level
Beginner

Finished Size
21 x 7 x 7-inch cylinder

Materials
- ⅔ yard 54-inch-wide decorator linen
- ½ yard 45-inch-wide synthetic suede
- Medium-weight fusible interfacing
- 1½ yards ¼-inch-diameter cotton cord
- Self-adhesive double-sided basting tape
- Permanent fabric glue
- Small amount polyester fibrefill
- 6 x 20-inch neck-roll pillow form
- 22 x 26-inch rectangle 1-inch-thick NU-Foam upholstery foam alternative
- Polyester fibrefill (optional)
- Basic sewing supplies and equipment

Cutting
From linen fabric:
- Cut one 22 x 25-inch rectangle.
- Cut two 8-inch-diameter circles.

From synthetic suede:
- Cut four 2½ x 22-inch strips for the bands.
- Cut two 1½ x 27-inch strips for the piping.
- Cut six ¾ x 15-inch strips for the ties.
- Cut one 5 x 20-inch strip for the opening insert.

From interfacing:
- Cut one 22 x 25-inch rectangle.
- Cut two 8-inch-diameter circles.

From cotton cord:
- Cut two 27-inch lengths.

Assembly
Notes: *Use ½-inch-wide seam allowances unless otherwise directed. Avoid using pins or ripping seams on the suede fabric, because the holes will show.*

1. Following the manufacturer's directions, fuse the interfacing to the wrong side of the corresponding linen pieces.

2. Use the cotton cord and the 1½ x 27-inch-wide suede strips to make piping by folding the suede strip over the cord (Figure 1) and straight-stitching. Trim cord as shown in Figure 2.

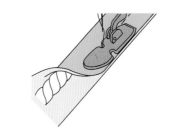

Figure 1

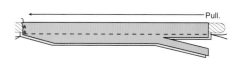

Figure 2

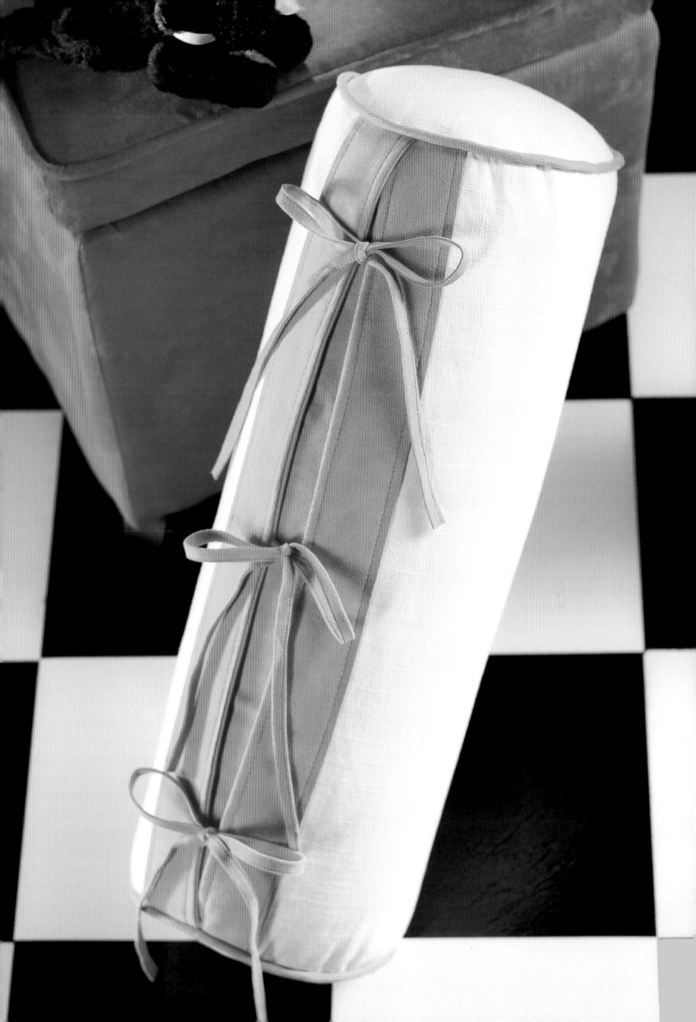

3. Use basting tape to apply the covered cord to the edge of each linen circle right side, with raw edges even and the cord toward the centre (Figure 3). Baste in place along the cord-cover basting line.

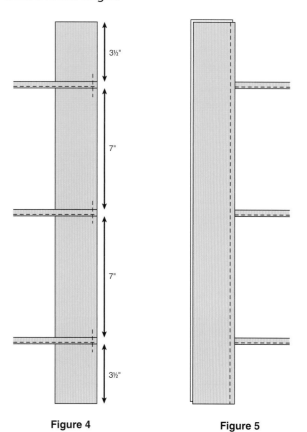

Figure 3

4. Fold each ¾ x 15-inch suede strip in half lengthwise with wrong sides facing and use basting tape to adhere the layers. Stitch close to the raw edges.
5. Edge-finish by placing one 2½ x 22-inch suede strip right side up on a flat surface. Position a tie at each of three locations as shown in Figure 4. Use basting tape to adhere the tie ends or stitch ¼ inch from the raw edges.

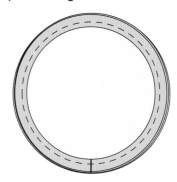

3½"

7"

7"

3½"

Figure 4

Figure 5

6. Place a second 2½ x 22-inch suede strip right side down over the strip with the ties. Use basting tape to hold it in place. Stitch ½ inch from the raw edges. Turn right side out and finger-press the seam, or use an iron with a press cloth to protect the fabric. Topstitch ¼ inch from the finished edge. Repeat with the remaining strips for the second edge finish (Figure 5).
7. Tuck each raw edge of the linen panel inside one of the suede bands with ties so the linen edge meets the suede seam-allowance edges inside. Use basting tape to secure both sides of the band to the linen. Topstitch ¼ inch from the suede raw edge (Figure 6).

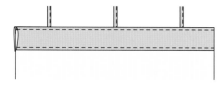

Figure 6

8. With right sides facing, pin a circle to each end of the linen panel with the suede band edges overlapping by about ½ inch. Position so the seam in the welting is opposite the band overlap (Figure 7). Stitch with the zipper foot adjusted to the right of the sewing machine needle.

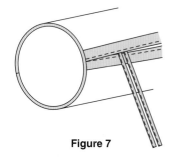

Figure 7

9. Wrap the pillow form with the upholstery foam alternative. Butt and glue the edges together with fabric adhesive. Allow the glue to dry thoroughly. Position the 5 x 20-inch suede strip on the roll on the side opposite from where the foam was glued. Glue in place.
10. Insert the form in the cover and adjust so the suede strip on the pillow is centred under the opening.
11. For rounder, smoother ends, use small bits of polyester fibrefill to stuff them to the desired roundness.
12. Tie the suede strips into bows. ◆

Hearts-All-Around Neck Roll

Pieced hearts and lace trim lend a romantic note to this pretty pillow. Coordinating purchased cord and tassels add the finishing flourishes.

DESIGN BY PAMELA LINDQUIST

Skill Level
Intermediate

Finished Size
Pillow: 6 x 18 inches

Materials
Note: *All yardages are for 44/45-inch-wide fabrics.*
- ¼ yard pink tone-on-tone fabric for the pieced upper heart section
- ¼ yard pink solid for the pieced lower heart section
- ⅜ yard cream tone-on-tone print for the heart block background
- ⅝ yard floral paisley print for the borders and bolster ends
- 1⅜ yards narrow lace trim
- 1⅜ yards ¼-inch-diameter pink corded piping for inner edge trim
- 1⅜ yards ½-inch-diameter pink corded piping for outer edge trim
- 6 x 18-inch bolster pillow form
- 2 (1-inch-diameter) decorative or self-covered buttons
- 2 decorative tassels
- Buttonhole twist or carpet thread for gathered end treatment (optional)
- All-purpose threads to match fabrics
- Rotary cutter, mat and ruler
- Zipper or piping foot
- Basic sewing supplies and equipment

Instructions
Notes: *Preshrink all fabrics. Strip lengths are based on 42 inches of usable width after preshrinking. If fabrics are narrower, you may need additional fabric. Measurements include ¼-inch-wide seam allowances unless otherwise stated.*

1. From the pink tone-on-tone print, cut two strips each 2½ x 42 inches; crosscut (30) 2½-inch squares. From the pink solid print, cut two strips each 2½ x 42 inches; crosscut 15 rectangles each 2½ x 4½ inches. From the cream tone-on-tone print, cut two strips each 1¼ x 42 inches; crosscut (60) 1¼-inch squares. Cut two strips each 2½ x 42 inches; crosscut (30) 2½-inch squares. From the floral paisley print, cut two strips each 3¾ x 20 inches and two strips each 4½ x 20 inches.

2. Using a sharp pencil and ruler, draw a diagonal line from corner to corner on the wrong side of each 1¼-inch cream square. Repeat with the 2½-inch cream squares.

3. With right sides together, place a marked 2½-inch cream square facedown at one end of a 2½ x 4½-inch pink rectangle. Stitch on the marked line. Trim the excess fabric ¼ inch from the stitching. Press the seam toward the cream triangle that remains. Repeat at the opposite end of the triangle. Repeat with the remaining cream squares and pink rectangles to make a total of 15 lower units (Figure 1).

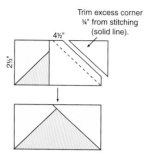

Trim excess corner ¼" from stitching (solid line).

4½"

2½"

Figure 1

4. Repeat Step 2 using the 1¼-inch cream squares and the 2½-inch pink squares to make a total of 30 quarter-heart units (Figure 2).

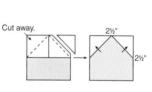

Cut away.

2½"

2½"

Figure 2   **Figure 3**

5. Sew the units from Step 4 together in pairs to make 15 half-heart upper units. Press the seam allowances to one side. Sew an upper heart unit to a lower unit to make 13 heart blocks (Figure 3). You should have two each of the upper and lower halves left.

6. Arrange the heart blocks and remaining half-heart units in three vertical rows as shown in Figure 4, beginning and ending the first and third rows with the half-heart units. Sew the blocks together in vertical rows and press the seams in opposite directions from row to row. Sew the rows together and press the seams in one direction.

Figure 4

7. Machine-baste lace trim to the long edges of the patchwork panel. Position the narrow corded piping at the long edges and machine-baste in place, using a zipper or piping foot to stitch close to the piping.

8. With right sides together, sew a 3¾ x 20-inch strip of floral paisley print to each long edge of the patchwork using the zipper foot to stitch close to the corded piping. Stitch from the patchwork side so you can see the stitching that holds the piping in place. **Note:** *It may feel like you are "crowding" the piping as you stitch but that is correct.* Press the seams toward the patchwork panel.

9. Fold the pillow cover in half crosswise with right sides together and the 19-inch-long raw edges even. Stitch ¼ inch from the edges and finger-press the seam open.

10. Turn the pillow cover right side out. Cut two 22-inch-long pieces of ½-inch-diameter pink corded piping. Using a ½-inch-wide seam allowance, sew the piping to the raw edges of each end of the pillow cover, angling the piping ends off the edge where they meet for a neat finish (Figure 5).

Figure 5

11. For the pillow ends, fold each 4½ x 20-inch strip of floral paisley print in half crosswise with right sides together and short raw edges even. Stitch ¼ inch from the raw edges.

12. Turn under and press ½ inch at one raw edge on each end piece and topstitch ¼ inch from the folded edge.

13. With right sides together, raw edges even and seam lines matching, pin one floral paisley print end piece to one open end of the pillow cover. Stitch ½ inch from the long edges. Repeat at the opposite end of the pillow cover.

14. Insert the pillow form.

15. Thread a hand-sewing needle with strong thread (buttonhole twist or carpet thread). Make running stitches along the finished edge of each end piece. Pull up the thread to gather and draw the ends into the centre. Tie off securely. Sew a large covered or purchased button in the centre at each end of the finished neck roll. Attach a tassel to each button. ◆

Flower Power

Here's a breezy bag that's so easy to sew you'll want to make several to coordinate with your favourite wardrobe pieces. Home dec fabrics offer great coordinates for the outer fabric and lining, but feel free to dress this bag up in quilted velvets, or try it in denim with a red drawstring for a more casual approach.

DESIGN BY CAROL ZENTGRAF

Skill Level
Easy

Finished Size
13 x 8 x 4 inches

Materials
- ⅓ yard floral print (home dec fabric; see Note at right)
- ⅓ yard plaid (home dec fabric)
- ⅜ yard nonwoven synthetic suede
- ⅓ yard 22-inch-wide heavyweight fusible interfacing
- 3 yards ¼-inch-diameter cotton filler cord
- 4 x 13-inch rectangle plastic needlepoint canvas for bottom support
- Temporary spray adhesive (optional)
- Air-soluble marking pen
- Permanent fabric adhesive
- Small, sharp scissors
- 14 gold grommets
- Grommet pliers
- All-purpose thread to match fabrics

- Basic sewing tools and equipment
Note: Home dec fabrics are heavier and have usually been treated for stain resistance, so they make great fabrics for handbags. If you choose other fabrics with less body, you can easily add support and weight by applying a fusible interfacing to the wrong side of the bag and lining pieces before you begin the construction.

Cutting
- Cut one 5 x 14-inch bag bottom and two 9½ x 18-inch bag bodies from the floral print and from the plaid fabric for the lining. Repeat with the interfacing.
- Following the manufacturer's directions, fuse the interfacing to the wrong side of the floral rectangles.

Assembly
Note: All seam allowances are ½ inch wide.
1. Staystitch a scant ½ inch from the lower edge of each large floral rectangle to reinforce the seam. Fold each piece in half crosswise and mark the

centre fold at the upper and lower edges. Fold the 5 x 14-inch floral strip in half crosswise and mark the centre fold at both long raw edges. Fold in half lengthwise and mark the centre at each short end.

2. With right sides facing, sew the short ends of the large floral rectangles together. Press the seams open (Figure 1).

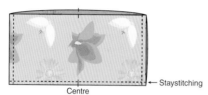

Centre ← Staystitching

Figure 1

3. With the centres of the short ends matching the side seams, and the centre front and centre back marks matching, pin the bag bottom to the bag front and back. Clip the bag to the staystitching at the corners as shown in Figure 2 so you can pivot and stitch smooth, square corners. Turn right side out and press.

Figure 2

4. Apply fabric adhesive around the inside bottom edges of the floral bag and put the needlepoint canvas panel in the bottom. Press it into the glue with your fingers and allow the glue to dry thoroughly.

5. Construct the lining from the plaid fabric following steps 1–3, but leave a 10-inch opening in one of the bottom long edges for turning. Do not turn right side out.

6. With right sides facing, place the floral bag inside the lining and stitch together around the upper edge. Trim the seam allowance to ¼ inch and carefully turn the bag right side out through the opening in the lining. Turn under and press the

lining opening edges; edgestitch together. Tuck the lining into the bag and press the upper edge. Topstitch ¼ inch from the upper edge.

7. Mark placement circles for three pairs of grommets on the bag front and back as shown in Figure 3. Mark a grommet placement circle over each side seam line, for a total of 14 grommets all around (Figure 3).

1" 2" 1" 2" 1"

Figure 3

8. Use the small, sharp scissors to cut small holes for the grommets. Follow the directions with grommet pliers to attach the grommets, placing the washers on the inside of the bag.

9. From the faux suede, cut enough 1½-inch-wide straight-grain strips to make a 108-inch-long strip. Sew the pieces together by overlapping the short ends and topstitching.

10. *Optional: Apply a light coat of temporary spray adhesive to the wrong side of the suede strip.* Centre the cotton filler cord on the wrong side of the strip and wrap the suede around the cord with the raw edges even. Attach the zipper foot and adjust the needle to the right of the foot. Stitch close to the cord and then trim the seam allowance close to the stitching.

11. For the drawstring, cut a 36-inch-long piece from the suede-covered cord. Beginning at one centre front grommet, weave the cord in and out of the grommets around the bag. Knot the ends, adjust the cord as desired and tie in a knot.

12. Thread the remaining suede-covered cord through the side grommets. Knot each cord end and then tie the cords together in an overhand knot 1½ inches from the ends. Position the knot at one side of the bag and adjust the straps to create a double handle. ✦

Denim Delight

Denim is always a winner, no matter your age or lifestyle. This hobo-style bag holds all your everyday needs in casual comfort.

DESIGN BY LINDA TURNER GRIEPENTROG

Skill Level
Easy

Finished Size
14½ x 14 inches

Materials
- ½ yard 44/45-inch-wide denim for bag
- ½ yard 44/45-inch-wide cotton print for lining
- ½ yard medium-weight fusible interfacing
- 1 pair 23-inch-long flat braided leather handles with rings
- 1 child's leather belt (22 to 24 inches, buckled length)
- All-purpose thread to match denim and lining
- Light brown topstitching or jeans thread
- Size 80/14 denim or jeans sewing machine needle
- Chalk marker
- Pattern-tracing paper
- Basic sewing supplies and equipment

Cutting
- Enlarge the bag pattern (Figure 1) on pattern-tracing cloth.
- From the denim, cut two bag bodies, one 2½ x 15-inch strip for the straps and one 1 x 26-inch strip for the loops.
- Turn under and press ¾ inch at the upper edge of the bag body pattern piece and cut two bag bodies and one 6 x 6-inch square for the inside pocket from the lining fabric.

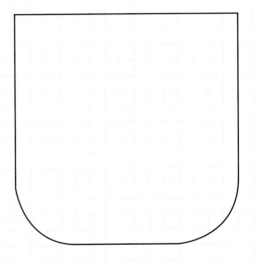

Figure 1
Bag Pattern
1 square = 1"

- From the interfacing, cut two bag bodies.

Assembly
Note: All seam allowances are ¼ inch wide, unless otherwise specified.

1. Fuse the interfacing to the wrong side of the denim bag bodies following the manufacturer's directions.

2. Turn under and press ¼ inch on three sides of the lining pocket square. Turn under and press ¼ inch at the upper edge and then turn again and press for a double hem. Topstitch the hem in place.

3. Centre and pin the pocket to one bag body

lining 6 inches from the upper edge; stitch in place along the side and bottom edges.

4. With right sides facing, sew the lining pieces together, leaving a 5-inch-long opening in the bottom seam for turning.

5. Turn under and press ¼ inch at each long edge of the 1-inch-wide denim strip for the belt loops. Fold in half lengthwise with the pressed edges even; stitch ⅛ inch from the long edges, using jeans thread in the size 80/14 needle. From the strip, cut nine 2½-inch-long belt loops.

6. Turn under and press ¼ inch at each end of each belt loop. On the bag front and back, draw a positioning line with the chalk marker 3½ inches from the upper raw edge. Position the loops on the bag body as shown in Figure 2. Topstitch in place at each short end. Use a short narrow zigzag stitch and backstitch at both ends.

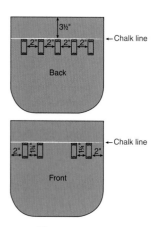

Figure 2

7. For the strap loops, turn under and press ¼ inch at each long edge of the 2½ x 15-inch denim strip. Fold in half lengthwise with the pressed edges even; tuck a strip of fusible web between the layers and fuse. Stitch ⅛ inch from the long edges, using jeans thread in the size 80/14 needle. From the strip, cut four 2½ x 3½-inch pieces. Loop each piece through a metal loop

of a braided strap and machine-baste the ends together ¼ inch from the raw edges.

8. Position the raw edges of the strap loops at the upper edge on the right side of the bag front and back 3½ inches from the sides (Figure 3). Take care not to twist the straps. Baste in place.

Figure 3

9. With right sides together, stitch the bag side and bottom seams, leaving an opening in the bottom edge for turning the bag right side out. Press the seams open, but do not turn the bag right side out.

10. Insert the lining into the bag with right sides facing and stitch the upper edges together. Make sure the strap loops are smooth and flat between the layers before stitching over them. Turn the bag right side out through the opening. Turn under and press the lining opening edges and edgestitch them together.

11. Tuck the lining into the bottom of the bag and press the upper edge. There should be a ¾-inch denim hem allowance. Topstitch ⅛ and ¼ inch from the upper edge, catching the strap loops in the stitching (Figure 4).

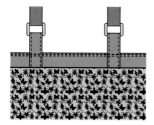

Figure 4

12. Thread the belt through the belt loops and buckle, pulling in the bag fullness as desired. ✦

Oh! Kimono!

This soft tote is the perfect place to showcase a collection of vintage kimono fabrics or some wonderful old ties.

DESIGN BY LINDA TURNER GRIEPENTROG

Skill Level
Easy

Finished Size
14½ x 14½ x 3 inches, excluding handles

Materials
Note: *Yardages are for 44/45-inch-wide fabrics.*
- ¾ yard silk dupioni for bag body
- ½ yard lining fabric
- ⅝ yard needled cotton quilt batting
- 2 (1¼ x 25-inch) strips of stiff interfacing, such as waistband interfacing, for the straps
- Assorted vintage kimono or tie fabrics for the patchwork, or substitute other fabrics of your choice
- All-purpose thread to match fabrics
- 1 (2-inch-long) Oriental charm
- 1 Chinese ball button
- 1 (3-inch-long) rayon tassel
- Temporary spray adhesive
- Air- or water-soluble marking pen
- Rotary cutter, mat and ruler
- Basic sewing supplies and equipment

Cutting
Notes: *Measurements include ¼-inch seam allowances unless otherwise stated. Cut the length of the tote pieces parallel to the selvages.*
- From the bag fabric, cut two 7 x 18-inch rectangles for the bag front, one 18-inch square for the bag back and two 3½ x 24-inch strips for the handles.
- From the lining fabric, cut two 16 x 18-inch rectangles.
- From the kimono fabrics, cut 9-inch-long strips in assorted widths from 1½–2½ inches wide. You will need enough strips for a finished 18-inch-long band. Strip-width variations add interest to the pieced band and allow you to cut around any stained or worn portions of the vintage fabric.
- From the quilt batting, cut two 18-inch squares.

Assembly
1. Arrange the kimono strips in the desired order and sew together using ¼-inch-wide seams. Press all seams in one direction.

2. Use rotary-cutting tools to trim the panel to 7 x 18 inches.

3. With right sides together, sew the 7 x 18-inch strips to the long edges of the kimono panel. Press the seams toward the pieced panel (Figure 1).

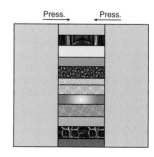

Figure 1

4. Apply a light coat of temporary spray adhesive to a piece of batting and smooth the bag front in place on top. Repeat for the bag back.

5. To make the bag handles, fold each 3½ x 24-inch silk strip in half and stitch the long edges together; turn right side out and press, centring the seam on the underside. Insert the stiff interfacing into the strip and trim the excess interfacing even with the strap ends. Topstitch ¼ inch from each long edge.

6. Position one handle on the bag front with raw ends even and the inner edges at the seam lines for the pieced panel. Machine-baste a scant ¼ inch from the raw edges. Edgestitch the handle to the bag front for 2 inches, pivot and stitch across the handle and then pivot again and stitch the remaining edge to the bag front (Figure 2). Position the remaining handle on the bag back, matching the positioning on the bag front. Stitch as you did for the front straps.

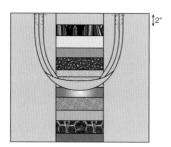

Figure 2

7. With right sides facing, sew the bag front to the back at the side and bottom edges. Press the seams open. Turn under and press a 2-inch-wide hem at the upper edge.

8. To box the bag bottom, align the side and bottom seam lines at each corner and pin. Draw a stitching line 1½ inches from the point. Stitch on the line and again ⅛ inch from the first stitching (Figure 3).

9. Trim the point close to the stitching. Do not turn the bag right side out.

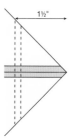

Figure 3

10. With right sides facing, sew the lining pieces together along the side and lower edges, but leave an 8-inch-long opening for turning. Finish the bottom corners as shown for the bag. Turn the lining right side out.

11. Tuck the lining inside the bag with raw edges even. Stitch. Turn the tote right side out through the opening in the lining.

12. Turn under and press the lining opening edges and machine-stitch the turned edges together. Tuck the lining into the bag and re-press the upper edge of the tote. **Optional:** Topstitch ¼ inch from the upper finished edge.

13. Sew the button, charm and tassel to the tote front as desired. ✦

Control Panels

If your kimono fabric is very lightweight or transparent, fuse tricot knit or lightweight weft-inserting interfacing to the underside before cutting into strips. This will prevent the seam allowances from showing through and give it comparable body to the other tote fabrics.

If you're using vintage ties for the pieced band, they're almost always cut on the bias, so it is essential to apply a lightweight nonwoven interfacing to the underside to control the stretch.

Coming Up Flowers Tote

Make this breezy summer handbag from home dec fabrics in your favourite florals. Punctuate it with a bold solid for the roomy gusseted pocket. Who says you can't take the garden with you?

DESIGN BY CAROL ZENTGRAF

Skill Level
Beginner

Finished Size
9 x 17 x 5 inches

Materials
- Firmly woven decorator fabric:
    - 13 x 34-inch rectangle floral print for handbag
    - 13 x 34-inch rectangle coordinating floral print for lining
    - 17 x 26-inch strip solid colour for pocket and closure
- 13 x 34-inch piece heavyweight fusible interfacing
- 1½ yards 1½-inch-wide striped taffeta ribbon
- 1½ yards 1½-inch wide coordinating striped grosgrain ribbon
- 1-inch-diameter button
- 1-inch-long strip ¾-inch-wide hook-and-loop tape
- ¼-inch-wide fusible web tape
- Point presser
- Basic sewing tools and equipment

Instructions
1. From each print and the interfacing, cut two 13 x 17-inch rectangles. Apply the fusible interfacing to the wrong side of the handbag rectangles, following manufacturer's directions.

2. From the solid fabric, cut one 17 x 22-inch rectangle for the pocket and one 4 x 6-inch strip for the tab closure.

3. Cut each ribbon into two equal lengths for the straps.

4. Fold the 17 x 22-inch pocket rectangle in half lengthwise, with wrong sides together, and press. Serge or machine-baste the side and bottom edges together. Use a marking pen to draw stitching lines and pleat fold lines on the panel as shown in Figure 1.

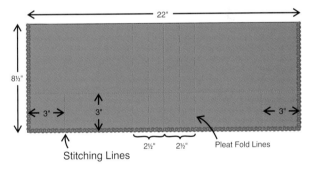

Figure 1

5. With the side and lower edges aligned, pin the pocket side edges to the handbag front panel. Make an inverted box pleat in the centre of the pocket as shown in Figure 2, and pin the lower edges to the panel. Keeping the folded edges of the pleat out of the way of the needle, topstitch the pocket to the handbag panel on the centre line. Topstitch through all layers on the remaining lines and along the lower 3 inches of each folded edge of the pleat. Machine-baste the pocket to the handbag panel ⅜ inch from the side and bottom edges.

Figure 2

6. With right sides together, sew the pocketed front panel to the back panel ½ inch from the side and bottom raw edges. Press the seams open on a point presser.

7. Fold the bag at each bottom corner with the bottom seam aligned with the side seam. Pin in place. Draw a line across the corner 3 inches from the point. Stitch on the line (Figure 3) and turn the bag right side out.

Figure 3

8. Repeat steps 6 and 7 to make the lining, but leave a 6-inch-long opening in the seam at the centre of the lower edge. Do not turn the lining right side out.

9. Place the handbag inside the lining with right sides together, and side seams and upper edges aligned; pin in place. Stitch ¼ inch from the upper raw edges. Turn the bag right side out through the opening in the lining. Turn under and press the seam allowances in the lining opening. Machine-stitch the folded edges together. Topstitch ½ inch from the upper edge of the bag.

10. For each handle, apply fusible web tape to the long edges on the wrong side of the striped ribbon. Remove the paper backing and position the striped ribbon on the grosgrain ribbon. Fuse in place following manufacturer's directions. Topstitch close to the long edges and down the centre of each strap. Turn under and press ½ inch at each short end of both pieces of ribbon and fuse in place with fusible tape.

11. Position the turned ends of the strap on the bag front 2 inches below the bag upper edge with 5 inches of space between the inner edges of the ribbon. Stitch in place along the side and lower edges and across the handle ½ inch from the upper edge of the bag. Sew the remaining handle to the bag back in the same manner (Figure 4).

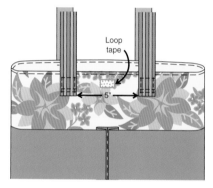

Figure 4

12. Fold the strip for the tab closure in half lengthwise with right sides together and stitch ¼ inch from the long edges. Press the seam open and arrange the seam in the centre of the strip. Stitch ¼ inch from one short end. Turn the strip right side out and press. Turn in and press ½ inch at the open end of the strip.

13. Position the pressed end of the strip 2 inches below the upper edge of the bag back, centring it between the strap ends. Stitch in place ¼ inch and ¾ inch from the pressed end. Sew the hook side of the hook-and-loop tape to the underside of the tab.

14. Sew the loop side of the tape to the centre of the bag front, ⅝ inch from the upper edge as shown in Figure 4. Sew the flower button to the right side of the closure. ◆

All Buttoned Up

This bag is the perfect size for the necessary items you might need for an evening out.

DESIGN BY PAMELA LINDQUIST

Skill Level
Easy

Finished Size
7 x 8 inches, excluding the handles

Materials
- ⅜ yard silk dupioni or other fabric for bag body
- ⅜ yard lining
- ⅜ yard light- to medium-weight fusible weft-insertion interfacing
- All-purpose thread to match fabrics
- 9 x 10-inch piece of pattern-tracing paper or cloth
- Air- or water-soluble marking pen
- Assorted white shell buttons, ¼–¾ inch in diameter
- 2 bangle bracelets (approximately ¼ inch thick) for bag handles
- Point turner for pressing
- Basic sewing supplies and equipment

Cutting
- Cut a 9 x 20-inch piece of interfacing and fuse to the wrong side of the bag fabric following the manufacturer's directions.
- Enlarge the bag pattern (Figure 1) on pattern-tracing paper or cloth and cut out. Use the pattern to cut two bag pieces each from the interfaced fabric and the lining. Cut one bag shape from the remaining interfacing and apply to the interfaced side of one of the bag pieces (bag back) so it has a double layer of interfacing.
- From the remaining un-interfaced bag fabric, cut two 1¼ x 22-inch strips for wrapping the bangles.

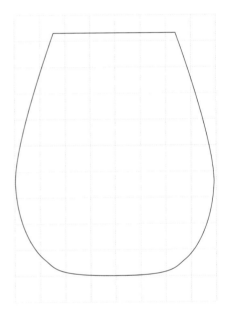

Figure 1
Pattern for All Buttoned Up
1 square = 1"

Assembly
Note: *Use ¼-inch-wide seam allowances throughout.*

1. On each bag and lining piece, machine-stitch a scant ¼ inch from the raw edges, beginning at the upper edge and continuing for a total of 5 inches from the upper edge (Figure 2).

2. With right sides together, sew a lining

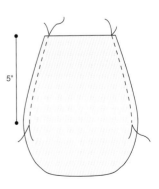

5"

Figure 2

piece to each bag piece, ending the stitching 3⅜ inches from the upper edge on each side. Clip the seam allowance at the end of the stitching (Figure 3). Slip the pieces over a point turner and press the seams open.

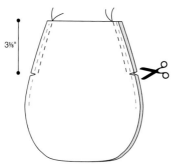

3⅜"

Figure 3

3. With right sides together, pin the bag pieces together and the lining pieces together. Stitch the pieces together (Figure 4). Turn right side out through the opening at the upper edge of the bag. Press as needed. Stitch the lining to the bag a scant ¼ inch from each upper raw edge.

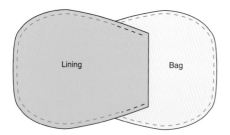

Lining   Bag

Figure 4

4. Arrange and sew the buttons to the bag front. Allow as little or as much of the bag fabric to show around the buttons and sew them in place through the bag layer only—not the lining. Buttons must end 1½ inches from the unfinished upper edge of the bag front (Figure 5).

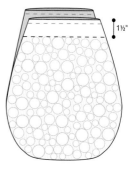

1½"

Figure 5

5. Turn under and press ¼ inch at each long edge of the fabric strips for the handles. Use the strips to wrap each bangle with fabric, overlapping the strips at an angle as you wrap. Cut away any excess strip and sew (or glue) the strip end in place.

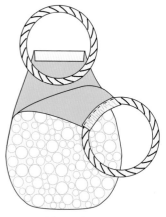

Figure 6

6. Turn under and press ¼ inch at each upper edge of the bag, using the stitching as a guide. With the raw end of the strip on the wrapped bangle toward the bottom of the bag, wrap the bag edge over a bangle and slipstitch the inner edge securely in place (Figure 6). Repeat with the remaining handle. ◆

Little Luxury

Combine bits of velvet, brocade and taffeta for a luxurious little evening bag.

DESIGN BY KAREN DILLON

Skill Level
Intermediate

Finished Size
7 x 10 inches, excluding straps

Materials
- ⅜ yard taffeta
- 6 x 16-inch piece velvet
- 6 x 8-inch scrap metallic brocade
- ¼ yard lining
- ¼ yard beaded fringe
- ½ yard narrow decorative cord
- 1¼ yards 1¼-inch-diameter twisted cord for strap
- 2 (8 x 12-inch) rectangles of cotton flannel for interlining
- 1 small decorative button
- Pattern-tracing paper or tissue
- Basic sewing supplies and equipment

Cutting
- From the taffeta, cut one 3½ x 26-inch rectangle and two 6½ x 7½-inch rectangles.
- From the velvet, cut two 6 x 7½-inch pieces.
- From the brocade, cut two 2½ x 6½-inch strips.
- Enlarge the pattern for the bag (Figure 1) on pattern-tracing paper or tissue and cut out. Use it to cut two pieces from the lining.
- From the flannel interlining, cut two 7½ x 11½-inch rectangles.

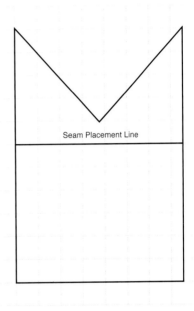

Figure 1
Bag Pattern
1 square = 1"

Seam Placement Line

Assembly
Note: All seam allowances are ¼ inch wide.

1. Working on a soft surface you can pin into, make random tapered tucks across the width of the 26-inch-long strip of taffeta. Pin tucks to the pinning surface as you make them and fold them from opposite edges so the wide ends of the uneven tucks alternate (Figure 2). Pleat the strip down to 6½ inches in length. Carefully readjust the pins so you can remove the piece from the pinning surface and stitch ⅛ inch from the long edges.

2. Centre the pleated panel on one 6½ x 7½-inch taffeta rectangle. Pin in place. With right sides facing, pin a brocade strip to one long edge of the pleated panel. Stitch ¼ inch from the long edges.

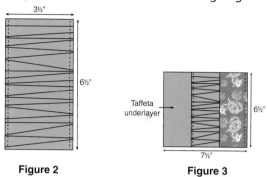

Figure 2

Taffeta underlayer →

Figure 3

Flip the brocade away from the pleats and press, using a press cloth to protect the fabrics (Figure 3). Do not press the pleats flat.

3. Add the remaining brocade strip to the opposite edge in the same manner. Machine-baste ⅛ inch from the long outer edges.

4. Cut two 6½-inch-long pieces of the narrow decorative cord and position them in the seam lines. Adjust the machine for a narrow zigzag stitch and couch the cords in place.

5. With right sides facing, pin one piece of velvet to the upper edge of the brocade/ pleated panel. Stitch ¼ inch from the raw edges. Hold the steam iron above the piece and use your fingers to press the seam toward the velvet. Sew the remaining piece of velvet to the upper edge of the remaining 6½ x 7½-inch rectangle and press in the same manner (Figure 4).

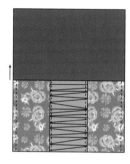

Figure 4

6. Place a flannel rectangle on the wrong side of each bag piece and pin in place. Place the bag pattern piece on top of each panel and pin in place with the placement line along the seam line. Cut out and then machine-baste ⅛ inch from all raw edges of each piece.

7. Cut a 7-inch-long piece of beaded fringe and centre it between the ¼-inch seam allowances at the lower edge of one of the bag pieces. Align the upper edge of the trim header with the lower raw edge of the bag, with the beaded fringe lying on the right side of the bag, pointing to the upper edge. Make sure the beads do not extend into the ¼-inch seam allowances at each side of the bag.

8. With right sides facing, sew the bag front and back together along the side and bottom edges. Press the side seams open over a point turner. Sew the lining pieces together in the same manner, leaving a 4-inch opening in the bottom seam for turning. Do not turn the lining right side out.

9. With raw edges even, pin the cord ends of the strap to the upper edges of the bag at the side seams. Check the cord length and adjust as needed. As cut, it is long enough to wear with the strap over your head so it crosses your chest. If that is too long, shorten the strap or tie the ends in an adjustable overhand knot. Baste the cord ends in place.

10. Tuck the bag inside the lining with upper raw edges even; stitch. When you are about 1 inch from a centre front or back point, shorten the stitch length and continue. At the point, pivot and stitch one or two small stitches, pivot again, stitch for an inch and then return to the normal stitch length until you are within 1 inch of the other point. Stitch and pivot in the same manner to complete the stitching (Figure 5).

Figure 5

11. Carefully turn the bag right side out through the opening in the lining. Turn under and press the opening edges in the lining and stitch them together. Tuck the lining into the bag and finger-press the upper edges with the help of a little steam from the iron. To keep the lining from rolling out at the upper edge, hand-stitch the lining to the seam allowance only. Tack the lining to the bag at the side seams. ◆

Lacy Bridal Wristlet

Scraps of lace and other bridal fabrics are perfect for this lovely bridal bag. A beaded tassel disguises the zipper pull on the lined bag that will hold the bride's essentials for the reception. Bridal attendants will love this bag, too, when made from fabrics that match or complement their gowns.

DESIGN BY BARBARA WEILAND

Skill Level
Intermediate

Finished Size
7 x 7 x 7 inches

Materials
- 7¾ x 15½-inch piece white silk dupioni or other bridal fabric
- 7¾ x 15½-inch piece white beaded lace
- 7¾ x 15½-inch piece very firm nonwoven fusible interfacing
- 7¾ x 15½-inch piece lining
- 14-inch-long piece white 1-inch-wide ribbon
- 7-inch white zipper
- 1 beaded tassel (about 2 inches long)
- White all-purpose thread
- Rotary cutter, mat and ruler
- Basic sewing tools and equipment

Assembly
1. Apply the firm interfacing to the wrong side of the silk dupioni following manufacturer's directions.

Note: *It may be necessary to add a second piece of interfacing on top of the first for the desired firmness so the bag holds its finished shape.*
2. Fold the piece in half crosswise and snip one edge at the fold. Position the short ends of the ribbon at the snip and machine-baste in place (Figure 1).

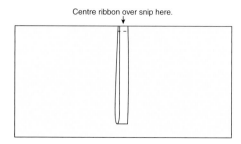

Centre ribbon over snip here.

Figure 1

3. *Unzip the zipper* and position face down on the right side of the silk with the bottom stop ½ inch from the short end of the rectangle. Using a zipper foot, stitch the zipper tape to the rectangle as shown in Figure 2.
4. Fold the piece in half crosswise with right sides together so you can position the other half of the zipper on the lace-covered silk with the bottom stop ½ inch from the remaining short end and

the upper ends of the two zipper tapes aligned. Stitch in place.

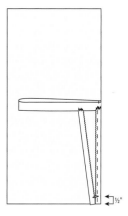

Figure 2

5. Press the fabric away from the zipper teeth, taking care to protect any beads or sequins on the lace from the heat of the iron (Figure 3).

Figure 3

6. Turn under and press ⅜ inch along one long edge of the lining. Position along the stitching on the wrong side of the zipper tape and slipstitch in place. Make sure the folded edge of the lining is away from the zipper teeth so that it won't get caught in the zipper sliding action. Machine-baste the lining raw

edges to the rectangle (trim away any excess lining to match the raw edges of the rectangle as needed). Zigzag-finish the long raw edge.

7. With the rectangle folded in half crosswise with right sides facing, stitch the edges opposite the zipper together (Figure 4). Press the seam open over a point presser and finish the seam edges with serging or zigzagging.

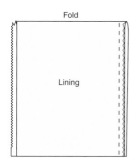

Figure 4

8. Unzip the zipper. With right sides together, align the seam line on one side with the zipper seam line on the other side of the bag; pin. Stitch ⅜ inch from the raw edges. Stitch again ⅛ inch from the first stitching. Trim the seam close to the second stitching (Figure 5).

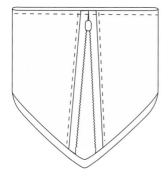

Figure 5

9. Turn the bag right side out and decorate the zipper pull with ribbon, tassels, or strands of pearls or beads as desired. ◆

Makeup in a Minute

Doing double or triple duty, this beautiful monogrammed makeup bag, jewellery holder or evening bag totes stuff in style. It's a great gift for any girlfriend on your list, or perfect for bridesmaids' gifts, monogrammed with the recipients' initials.

DESIGN BY LINDA TURNER GRIEPENTROG

Skill Level
Intermediate

Finished Size
10 x 6½ x 2 inches

Materials
- 44/45-inch-wide silk dupioni:
    - ⅜ yard solid for bag
    - ⅜ yard coordinating print for underlining
- Lightweight batting
- 10-inch zipper
- Bias tape for finishing seams
- Rayon machine-embroidery thread
- Tassel for zipper pull
- Tear-away stabilizer
- Quilting guide
- Machine-embroidery alphabet with 3½–4-inch-tall lettering
- Embroidery machine
- Temporary spray adhesive
- Basic sewing supplies and equipment

Quilting
1. Spray batting with temporary adhesive and layer between wrong sides of bag fabric and underlining fabric.

2. Thread machine with rayon machine-embroidery thread. Select an open-artwork decorative machine stitch. Working from the centre out and using the quilting guide to maintain even widths between stitching rows, machine-quilt parallel lines vertically across width of fabric, spacing 1 inch apart.

Cutting
From quilted fabric for bag:
- Cut one 16¼ x 11-inch rectangle.
- Use pattern provided to cut two bag ends.

Embroidery
1. Using embroidery software on on-screen editing, assemble desired lettering for monogram. Vary style, size and positioning as desired.

2. Print a full-size design template and mark the embroidery placement lines on the front half of the bag body rectangle.

3. Hoop tear-away stabilizer; spray with temporary adhesive. Position bag body rectangle, matching design placement lines to marked monogram location.

4. Embroider monogram. Trim jump threads and remove stabilizer according to manufacturer's instructions.

Assembly

Note: *Use ½-inch-wide seam allowances.*

1. Bind short straight edges of bag body rectangle with bias tape. ***Note:*** *If preferred, leave seams unfinished and line bag following instructions in sidebar below.* Press finished edges under ½ inch. Sew zipper to pressed edges, keeping the stop at least ½ inch from one end to allow for seaming (Figure 1).

Figure 1

2. With right sides together, sew bag ends to body, clipping corners as needed to create a smooth seam (Figure 2).

Figure 2

3. Trim end seams and bind with bias tape to finish. Turn bag right side out. Attach tassel to zipper pull. ✦

Lined Bag

Cut one 16¼ x 11-inch rectangle and two bag ends from suitable lining fabric. Sew together as for monogrammed bag, omitting the zipper. Place lining inside bag and hand-stitch around top opening.

Bag End Template
Cut 2

Just Call Me Cellphone Caddies

Let your phone be cradled in soft pretty surroundings while you wait for that special someone to call.

DESIGNS BY KELLY LAWRENCE

Skill Level
Intermediate

Finished Sizes
Pretty in Pink: 3 x 4 inches
Fashion-Oriented Calls: Approximately 3⅜ x 4 inches

Materials for Pretty in Pink
• 5 x 10-inch piece embroidered or printed pink sheer
• 5 x 10-inch piece matching lining fabric
• ½ yard twisted pink cord for strap

Materials for Fashion-Oriented Calls
• 5 x 9-inch piece red brocade
• 5 x 9-inch piece red lining
• 5 x 9-inch piece fusible fleece (fusible on one side)
• 8 faceted rondelle beads for handle
• Clear nylon monofilament thread
• Craft glue

For Both Projects
• Basic sewing supplies and equipment

Pretty in Pink

Instructions
Note: *Before beginning, read Customize It and adjust the dimensions for the bag as required to fit your phone.*

1. Trim the fabric and lining pieces to 4¼ x 9 inches.
2. With right sides facing, stitch the lining to the fabric ¼ inch from each short end. Turn the piece right side out and fold in half with the raw edges even. Press lightly to mark the bottom crease. Unfold the piece and machine-baste along the crease.
3. Fold the bag in half with the lining inside and raw edges even. Stitch ⅜ inch from the raw edges. Press the seam allowances open on a point turner and trim to ⅛ inch. Re-press the seam allowances together.
4. Fold the cord in half to form a doubled 9-inch-long piece. Position the cord with the ends ⅜ inch from the upper edge as shown in Figure 1;

Customize It

Before you cut the pieces for your phone, check the measurements of your cellphone and adjust the cutting dimensions as needed so the caddy will fit it to perfection.
1. Measure the phone circumference with a tape measure and add ½ inch for a snug fit or ¾ inch for a looser fit. Add 1 inch for the side seam allowances.
2. Measure the cellphone length and add 1 inch for seam allowances.

machine-stitch across the cord ends, stitching them to the seam allowance only at each side of the bag.

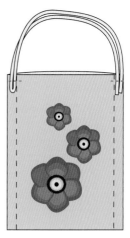

Figure 1

5. Turn the bag wrong side out, press along the seam lines and stitch ¼ inch from the seamed edges, enclosing the raw edges of the first seam to make self-finished French seams.

6. With right sides together, align one side seam line with the row of basting at the bag bottom to form a point. Stitch ½ inch from the point. Repeat at the remaining corner to box the bottom (Figure 2). Turn the completed bag right side out.

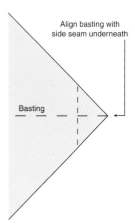

Align basting with
side seam underneath

Basting

Figure 2

7. Remove the basting and tuck your cellphone inside.

Fashion-Oriented Calls

Instructions

1. Fold the brocade and lining pieces in half crosswise and trim as shown in Figure 3.

4½"

5"

Figure 3

2. Repeat step 1 with the fleece. Unfold and trim ½ inch from each long edge and ¼ inch from each short edge to eliminate bulk in the seams. Centre the fleece on the wrong side of the brocade piece and fuse in place.

3. With the lining and brocade right sides together, stitch ¼ inch from the short ends. Turn right side out and press.

4. Fold the bag in half with the lining inside and raw edges even. Stitch ⅜ inch from the raw edges. Press the seam allowances open on a point turner and trim to ⅛ inch. Turn the bag wrong side out, press along the seam lines and stitch ¼ inch from the seamed edges, enclosing the raw edges of the first seam to make self-finished French seams. Press the seams to one side and topstitch ⅛ inch from the upper edge of the bag.

5. Thread a sewing needle with clear nylon monofilament thread and double it. Take several small stitches in place at one seam allowance to anchor the thread. Add 48 beads. Take another stitch at the opposite seam allowance inside the bag, and then thread the needle back through the beads. Draw up the thread so the beads form a handle and take several stitches in place at the first seam. For added security, make a dressmaker's knot in the thread and add a dot of craft glue. ✦

Travel in Style Luggage Set

You'll be travelling in style when you make this coordinating set from home decor-weight fabrics. The garment bag is large enough to hold several hanging ensembles and has handles for easy carrying. The tote features a sturdy base and inside pockets.

DESIGNS BY CAROL ZENTGRAF

Skill Level
Intermediate

Finished Size
24 x 53 x 3½ inches

Materials
- 45-inch-wide home decor fabric:
    3 yards print for outer bag
    3 yards coordinating print for lining
- ⅔ yard fusible interfacing
- ⅜ yard extra-wide double-fold bias tape
- 36-inch zipper
- ¼-inch-wide double-stick fusible web tape
- Basic sewing supplies and equipment

Garment Bag

Cutting
From fabric for outer bag:
- Cut one 25 x 54-inch rectangle for back. To shape the corners, fold rectangle in half with right sides together. On one short end, draw a gently curving line from the fold to 9 inches below the opposite corner. Cut along the marked line through both layers. Use the shaped end as a guide to cut the corners on the opposite end to match.
- Cut two 13 x 54-inch rectangles for fronts. Round outer corners to match back.
- Cut three 4½ x 48-inch strips for sides.
- Cut two 5 x 24-inch strips for straps.

From coordinating fabric for lining:
- Cut one 25 x 54-inch rectangle for back. Round corners to match outer bag back.
- Cut two 13 x 54-inch rectangles for fronts. Round outer corners to match back.
- Cut three 4½ x 48-inch strips for sides.

From the fusible interfacing:
- Cut two 5 x 24-inch strips.

Assembly
Note: Use ½-inch-wide seam allowances and sew seams with right sides together unless otherwise indicated.

1. Sew the straight edges of the outer bag front pieces together for 2 inches at the upper edge. Leave a 36-inch opening for the zipper, and then sew the edges together to the bottom of the bag.

2. Following manufacturer's instructions, apply fusible web tape to the right side of the zipper opening edges; do not remove the paper backing. Press the opening edges under ½ inch. With the front right side up, place the zipper right side up under the opening. Remove the paper backing from the fusible web and adhere to the zipper tape; the folded edges should meet in the centre of the zipper. Fuse in place.

3. Repeat steps 1 and 2 for the front lining pieces, adhering the opening seam allowances to the wrong side of the zipper; the outside and lining should have wrong sides together. Using a zipper foot, sew the zipper tapes in place, continuing the stitching along the seam lines above and below the zipper. Serge or zigzag-stitch the edges of the outer front and lining together.

4. With wrong sides together, serge or zigzag-stitch the edges of the outer bag back and lining back pieces together.

5. Stitch the short edges of the outer bag sides together making a long strip of fabric. Repeat for the lining sides. With wrong sides together, serge or zigzag-stitch the edges of the outer and lining sides together. Bind one short edge of the side with a 5-inch length of bias tape.

6. Fuse the interfacing to the wrong sides of the strap pieces. On the interfacing side of each strap, fuse web tape along all edges. Using the paper backing as a guide, press all edges ½ inch to the interfacing side. Remove the backing. Fuse the short edges and then the long edges in place. Press each strap in half lengthwise. Edgestitch the open folded edges together, then edgestitch along the three remaining edges. Stitch along the lengthwise centre of each strap.

7. On the right side of the back piece, pin the straps to each end with the short edges 4½ inches from the end and spaced 5½ inches apart. Securely stitch the straps in place along the stitching lines to 2 inches from the bag end.

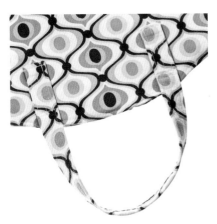

8. Align the bound edge of the bag side with the top of the bag front, outside fabrics together, and pin. Continue pinning the side strip around the front, with edges even, to 2 inches from the beginning point. Overlap the beginning end ¼ inch and cut the excess side. Bind this edge with bias tape as before. Continue pinning the side to the front. Sew the side to the front.

9. Partially unzip the zipper. Pin, and then sew the side strip to the back with outside fabrics together. Turn right side out.

10. Press the edges to crease at the seam lines. Fold the side edges along the seam lines and stitch ¼ inch from the edge.

Tote Bag

Finished Size
24 x 14 x 8 inches

Materials
- 45-inch-wide home decor fabric:*
    - 1½ yards print for outer bag
    - 1½ yards coordinating print for lining
- 1½ yards fusible interfacing
- ¼ yard stiff heavyweight interfacing
- ¼-inch-wide double-stick fusible web tape
- Permanent fabric adhesive
- Basic sewing supplies and equipment

Model project was made using Michael Miller Fabrics Cabana Collection #3095 Dandy Damask/Spa for the outer bag and CO#3359 Feeling Groovy/Spa for the lining.

Cutting
From print fabric for outer bag:
- Cut two 25 x 15-inch rectangles for front and back. To shape bag front and back pieces, make a mark on the lower edge 1 inch from each side. Draw a line from each upper corner to this mark. The upper edge will be 25 inches wide, and the lower edge will be 23 inches wide.
- Cut one 9 x 15-inch rectangle for base.
- Cut one 10 x 20-inch rectangle for outer pocket.
- Cut two 5 x 54-inch strips for handles.

From coordinating print fabric for lining:
- Cut two 25 x 15-inch rectangles for front and back. Shape in same manner as for outer bag.
- Cut one 9 x 15-inch rectangle for the base.
- Cut one 18 x 24-inch rectangle for inside pocket.

From interfacing:
- Cut two 25 x 15-inch rectangles for front and back. Shape in same manner as for outer bag.
- Cut two 5 x 54-inch strips for handles.

From stiff interfacing:
- Cut one 8 x 14-inch rectangle for base.

Assembly
Note: *Use ½-inch-wide seam allowances and sew seams with right sides together unless otherwise indicated.*

1. Fold lining inside pocket rectangle in half crosswise and press. Pin to the right side of lining back, aligning bottom raw edges. Trim sides of the pocket to match the lining piece and baste in place. Pin the folded edge of the pocket to the lining.
2. Sew the side seams of the lining front and back together.
3. Fuse interfacing to the wrong side of each outer bag front and back. Fold outer pocket rectangle in half crosswise and press. Pin to the centre of the bag front with lower raw edges even. Baste the side and lower edges of the pocket in place.
4. Sew side seams of outer bag front and back together.
5. With right sides together, place the outer bag in the lining, aligning side seams and upper and lower edges. Sew together along upper edges. Turn the lining inside the bag and press the edge. Topstitch ¼ inch from the edge.
6. Follow step 6 of the garment bag to make the straps.
7. Referring to photo for placement, pin one strap to the front of the bag, covering the side edges of the pocket and aligning the ends of the strap with the bottom edge of the bag front. Sew the strap in place to the upper edge of the bag, stitching along the strap stitching lines. Sew the second strap to the back of the bag, aligning the placement with the strap on the bag front. **Note:** *The strap stitching will create divisions in the inside pocket.*
8. On the outside base piece, mark the centre of each short end with a pin. Turn the bag inside out. Aligning the pin marks with the side seams of the bag, pin, and then sew the base piece in place. Turn right side out and press.
9. Glue the edges of the base lining piece around the stiff heavyweight interfacing rectangle. Place the base inside the bag with the covered side up. Glue edges in place. ◆

Wintry Pines
Continued from page 32

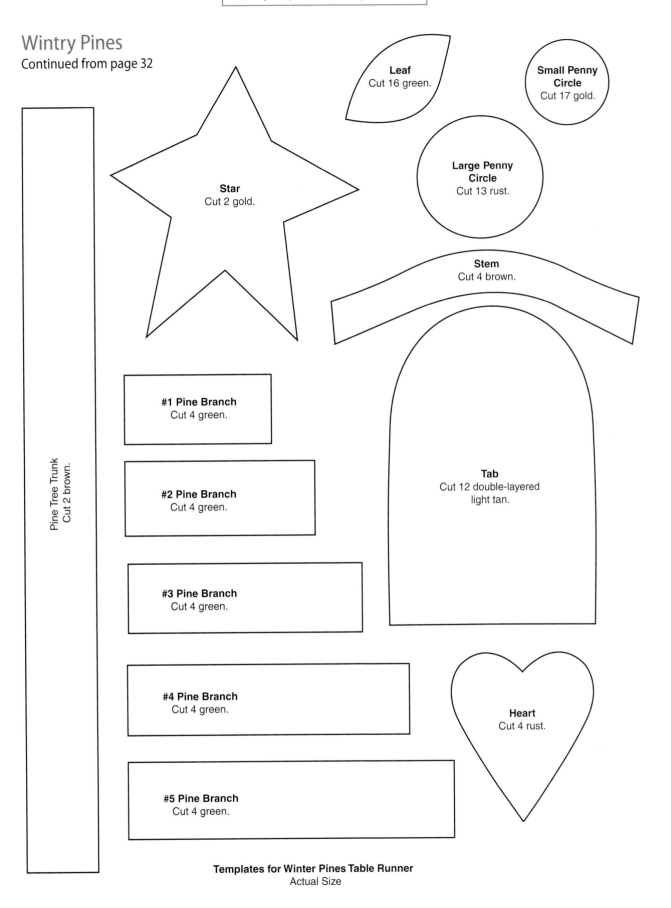

Leaf
Cut 16 green.

Small Penny Circle
Cut 17 gold.

Star
Cut 2 gold.

Large Penny Circle
Cut 13 rust.

Stem
Cut 4 brown.

Pine Tree Trunk
Cut 2 brown.

#1 Pine Branch
Cut 4 green.

#2 Pine Branch
Cut 4 green.

#3 Pine Branch
Cut 4 green.

#4 Pine Branch
Cut 4 green.

#5 Pine Branch
Cut 4 green.

Tab
Cut 12 double-layered light tan.

Heart
Cut 4 rust.

Templates for Winter Pines Table Runner
Actual Size

INDEX

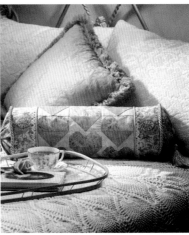